Royal Horticultural Society

Garden Ideas

MONTH BY MONTH

Royal Horticultural Society

Garden Ideas
MONTH BY MONTH

ZIA ALLAWAY

LIA LEENDERTZ

Editor Zia Allaway
Designer Alison Shackleton
Pre-Production Producer
Rebecca Fallowfield
Senior Producer Charlotte Oliver
Special Sales Creative Project Manager
Alison Donovan
Photography Brian North, Peter Anderson

RHS Publisher Rae Spencer-Jones

First published in Great Britain in 2015 by
Dorling Kindersley Limited,
80 Strand, London WC2R 0RL

Material previously published as:
How To Grow Practically Everything (2010)

Copyright © 2010, 2015 Dorling Kindersley Limited

A Penguin Random House Company
001–290700–Oct/2015

A CIP catalogue record for this book is available
from the British Library

ISBN 978-0-2412-4760-0

Printed and bound in Italy

To find out more about RHS membership, contact:
RHS Membership Department,
PO Box 313, London, SW1P 2PE
Telephone: 0845 062 1111; www.rhs.org.uk

IMPORTANT NOTICE
The authors and the publisher can accept no liability for
any harm, damage, or illness arising from the use or
misuse of the plants described in this book.

A WORLD OF IDEAS
SEE ALL THERE IS TO KNOW

www.dk.com

Contents

page
8

page
42

page
85

page
108

How plants grow

One of the pleasures of gardening is that it gives you the chance to watch nature at work. As soon as you put a plant in the ground, a cycle of growth and reproduction begins. Learn what plants need to grow strong and healthy, and you can help them to put on their best performance.

Vital supplies

Plants need water, air, nutrients, and light to thrive, and when first planted they are dependent on you to provide them. Neglect them at this stage and they are unlikely to survive.

LIGHT REQUIREMENTS

Plants make energy from sunlight through photosynthesis, and only thrive if they receive the right amount for their needs. Different plants have evolved to survive in different conditions, and while some love shade, others prefer their heads in the sun. Plants also offer clues about the conditions they enjoy — those with small hairy or grey leaves, such as lavender, enjoy sunny sites, and those with large, dark green leaves grow well in shade. When choosing plants, check their light requirements and plant them in an appropriate place. Young plants are particularly vulnerable to poor light conditions and will struggle to establish if the sun is blocked by weeds, so keep the area around them free of competing plants as they mature.

REGULAR WATER SUPPLIES

When young, all plants need regular watering because their small root systems are unable to search for moisture if it doesn't come to them. You can encourage your plants to develop deep, self-sustaining root systems by watering occasionally but deeply, using one large watering can-full per plant. Moisture then seeps deep into the soil, and the roots reach down to find it.

SOIL NEEDS

Plants love to sink their roots into aerated, moist yet well-drained soil. To achieve these ideal conditions, dig in plenty of organic matter, such as well-rotted manure or mushroom compost before planting, and spread a thick layer on the soil surface in spring. Earthworms will then drag it down into the soil, where it will gradually improve drainage and water-retention capacity, ensuring your soil contains all the nutrients and moisture necessary for seeds to germinate and roots to explore.

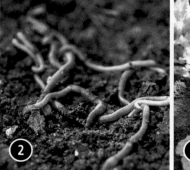

❶ Sunflowers literally love their heads in the sun and their blooms follow its path throughout the day. ❷ Earthworms produce gums that bind soil particles together, helping to improve soil structure. ❸ Water young plants regularly to help their roots to establish.

∧ Hungry roots
The area close to the root tips is covered in tiny hairs that absorb nutrients dissolved in the soil water. Take care not to damage these.

FOOD FOR THOUGHT

Plants feed via their roots, removing minerals dissolved in water in the soil. They are constantly seeking new areas to exploit and form a large underground network, so that when one area dries out or is killed off, other roots can be relied upon to take over and keep the plant alive. In a natural environment, the plant population will adjust to the nutrients that are available. In a well-stocked garden where plants are growing closely together you will need to top-up the nutrient level regularly by applying fertilizer and organic matter, such as well-rotted manure.

Organic fertilizers are a good choice for borders, as they release nutrients slowly, feeding plants for a season, and do not harm beneficial soil organisms. You can also apply fertilizer directly to the leaves with a foliar feed. If a plant is suffering from a trace element deficiency, such as iron or manganese, a spray of foliar fertilizer can quickly improve its health. Apply fertilizer to the backs of leaves where they can absorb it more easily.

How plants reproduce

Every plant is designed to ensure its survival or that of the next generation, but they go about it in different ways. Some produce copious amounts of seed, while others reproduce vegetatively, extending their root systems through the soil.

MAKING SEED

Plants with colourful, nectar-filled flowers attract pollinating insects that pick up pollen from one flower and transfer it to another. This process activates plants' sexual reproduction, and prompts the flowers to start developing into seeds. The benefit of reproducing sexually is that every seedling has a slightly different genetic make-up, and when adverse conditions hit, only the fittest survive to breed again, strengthening the species.

ROOTING AROUND

Many creepers and climbers throw out long stems above ground that produce roots when they touch the soil. The roots of others clump up and spread gradually, while some send up shoots from long, extended roots. The danger of vegetative reproduction is that it produces a less diverse population, which is more vulnerable to changing conditions. This is why plants that reproduce asexually also flower and set seed, just in case.

1 Insects, such as bees, transfer pollen from one plant to another, which activates sexual reproduction. **2** The male pollen grains fertilize female parts of the flower, stimulating the production of seeds. **3** The arching shoots of brambles start to grow roots when they touch the soil, producing a new plant. **4** Bamboos throw out long underground roots called "runners", which in turn generate shoots that grow to form new plants.

Striking stems

Many dogwood and willow varieties have brightly coloured stems that are a boon in the winter garden. The young growth is the most impressive, so prune hard to encourage bright new shoots.

Willow wands

Willows (*Salix*) look great grown as pollards. Let a single stem grow to about 1.5m (5ft) tall, and prune so that new growth develops at the top, creating a head of colourful young stems.

>> **WHEN TO START**
Late winter or early spring
AT ITS BEST
Winter

TIME TO COMPLETE
 1 hour
YOU WILL NEED
 Willow plant
Secateurs
Loppers or pruning saw
All-purpose granular fertilizer

2 **PRUNE TO ONE OR TWO BUDS**
Before new growth appears in spring, use secateurs to cut back every stem to one or two buds. Use a pruning saw to remove larger material.

3 **AFTER PRUNING**
The shrub will look strange after pruning but don't panic; it will quickly re-grow. Give it an annual feed of all-purpose granular fertilizer, worked into the soil around the base of the plant. Use the cut stems to support perennials in spring and summer.

1 **REMOVE WEAK GROWTH**
When the leaves fall in autumn, tidy the plant by carefully pruning out weak and damaged stems, and remove any shoots from the main trunk.

Dramatic dogwoods

Dogwoods (*Cornus* species) are grown for their bare winter stems, which can be green, red, orange, or bright yellow. The youngest growth is the most vibrant, so prune them almost to the ground every year to encourage new stems.

1 ANNUAL PRUNING
In late winter or early spring, prune dogwoods back by cutting all stems to one or two buds above the ground. Use secateurs for the thinner stems, and loppers or a pruning saw for larger ones.

2 LEAVE AN OPEN STRUCTURE
New stems will grow from the top buds left behind. If there are several buds, remove those facing into the centre of the plant by rubbing them off with your fingers. This stops the new stems becoming too congested, which will weaken the winter display.

3 ALTERNATIVE APPROACH
Instead of pruning your dogwoods entirely to the ground, you can prune out every third stem. The plant will look less scalped through the summer, although the winter show will not be as dramatic as a result.

< Bare essentials
Plant spring-flowering bulbs beneath your dogwoods and willows to give an extra splash of colour.

Weave a living willow screen

Slimmer than a hedge and just as easy to create, willow screens are ideal for partitioning small gardens or as boundaries in rural settings where you want a barrier that mirrors the natural landscape beyond. Once established, they also make good windbreaks for a vegetable plot or flower garden.

 WHEN TO START
Winter, when willow is dormant
AT ITS BEST
All year round

TIME TO COMPLETE
 4–5 hours over a few months

YOU WILL NEED
 Willow setts
Well-rotted organic matter,
 such as farmyard manure
Spade
Garden tarred twine
Rubber plant ties

 GROW OR BUY WILLOW
The most common willow for weaving is *Salix alba*, which has colourful stems in winter. Buy your cuttings or "setts" in winter and plant as soon as possible. Do not plant near buildings or drainage pipes, as the roots are invasive.

PLANT SETTS
Dig plenty of organic matter into the soil and remove weeds. Push a spade into the soil 20cm (8in) deep, insert a willow sett into the slit and firm in. Space setts 20cm (8in) apart. Water well. Wait until new growth appears before weaving.

WEAVE THE WILLOW
Criss-cross the stems over and under one another to form a rigid diamond-shaped structure. Tie stems where they cross with twine, and use rubber plant ties to secure the top of the screen. This allows some movement and prevents stems from snapping in the wind.

TOP TIP: BUYING AND CARING FOR WILLOW

The easiest way to buy willow cuttings is from a specialist willow nursery – most now have online and mail-order shops. The cuttings are harvested when dormant in winter, and will only be available at this time. They are normally 20–30cm (10–12in) long and take a season to grow to a suitable length for weaving. Rods for tunnels are longer. Keep the growing area free of weeds and water the cuttings well after planting and until they are fully established.

Make a tunnel

Natural and inexpensive, this willow tunnel takes no longer to make than a screen, and can be used for children's play areas or in a cottage or informal design. To create a living tunnel, buy longer "rods" instead of setts or cuttings.

1 MARK OUT THE SITE
Prepare the site and soil as for screens (*see opposite*). Measure the length of the tunnel and calculate the number of rods you will need: they are planted in pairs 30cm (12in) apart, or closer if you want a dense effect. You will also need a few spares. When the rods arrive, plant as for setts (*see opposite*), but in slits that are 30cm (12in) deep.

2 FORM THE ARCH
Plant rods in matching pairs on either side of your marked-out tunnel. Bend each pair over to form an arch and twist them together. Secure with rubber plant ties. Plant some rods between the other stems and weave them across the structure to help strengthen it. Tie these rods on either side of the arch stems, as shown above.

3 FINAL TOUCHES
Water well and apply a mulch each spring. Keep the arch well watered for the first year and weed regularly.

TOP TIP: PRUNING AND AFTERCARE

To top up moisture levels, consider installing a leaky hose beside the arch, which can be attached to an automatic timer. Remove any dead plants as you see them and replant with fresh ones. Do not trim your hedge or arch until the end of the first year when the leaves have dropped. Once well established, willow structures will produce long shoots, which you can cut back and chip for use as a mulch or as fuel for a woodburner. Alternatively, you can plant these "cuttings" to make more willow structures.

Elegant standards

Standard trees make a bold statement in the garden but can be expensive to buy, but with a little patience and the right care you can create your own, as long as the plant has a strong lead shoot.

 WHEN TO START
Anytime

AT ITS BEST
All year round

TIME TO COMPLETE

 Initial pruning, 30 minutes

YOU WILL NEED

 A variegated holly, such as
Ilex x *altaclerensis* 'Golden King'
used here
Large container
Garden cane
Twine
Secateurs

1 ASSESS THE PLANT
Look at the plant from all angles before pruning. Decide how long you want the clean stem to be and what growth you are going to leave to make up the lollipop top.

2 REMOVE SIDE SHOOTS
Prune the lowest side shoots from the main stem, but don't remove them all in one go as they help to pull sap up the plant. Once the plant has a decent round head, you can cut them all off.

3 TIE IN AND SHAPE
Shorten the growth left at the top of the plant slightly to encourage it to bush out and form a rounded head. Push a cane into the compost to support the main stem, which will be quite weak at this early stage; tie securely in several places. Trim the head to shape each year.

Planting options

Almost any shrub can be grown as a standard, and if you have the time it is worth experimenting to see which work best.

GLOBES OF FLOWERS AND FOLIAGE

Roses are traditionally trained as standards, and are particularly effective grown in this formal way with less traditional mixed cottage-style planting beneath them. The same is true of wisterias. Other commonly grown standard lollipop trees include box and bay, often used for topiary, and decorative evergreens, such as rosemary, *Euonymus fortunei,* and *Photinia*. You can also create interesting foliage and structural effects with large deciduous trees, such as acers and oaks, trimmed into standards, as long as you prune them regularly.

❶ *Rosmarinus officinalis* has silvery growth and looks good rising above a planting of cool whites and purples.
❷ *Euonymus fortunei* provides brightly coloured variegated foliage all year round, even in shady corners.
❸ *Photinia* x *fraseri* 'Red Robin' is green all year but produces a flush of bronze-red new foliage every spring.

< *Holly head*
Variegated holly, shaped into a standard tree, brings strong colour, structure and style to any mixed planting or group of containers.

Plant fruit in a small space

Even if you have no garden soil in which to plant, you can still grow a fruit tree if you make your choice carefully. Almost all fruit trees can be bought grown on dwarfing rootstocks, and are happy in large containers, as long as they're well watered and fed. Such small trees can be surprisingly bountiful.

〉〉 **WHEN TO START**
Late winter
AT ITS BEST
Autumn

TIME TO COMPLETE
🕐 1 hour

YOU WILL NEED
🔋 A large pot
Broken clay pot pieces
John Innes No.3 compost
Slow-release granular fertilizer
A dwarf fruit tree
Pebbles or chips for mulch

1 BEFORE PLANTNG
Fruit trees grown in containers are almost totally dependent on the fertilizer and water you give them. So, to give your tree the best start and to help it establish, soak the root ball before planting, as it is hard to wet dry roots thoroughly afterwards. The best way to do this is to immerse the pot in a large bucket of water and leave it to soak for about an hour, or until the soil surface is damp. Then, lift the tree from the bucket and allow it to drain.

2 PREPARE TO PLANT
Choose a large pot with a wide base so that the tree is not easily blown over, and stand it in a sunny, sheltered spot. Make sure it has plenty of drainage holes, or drill your own, and cover them with a layer of broken clay pot pieces to prevent compost blocking them up. Fill the base with compost, and add a sprinkling of slow-release fertilizer.

3 TEASE OUT ROOTS
Place the tree in the pot, adding or removing compost, until the top of the root ball is about 5cm (2in) below the rim. Then lift the plant, remove its original pot, and tease out the roots from the root ball. This encourages the roots to grow out into the compost, stabilizing the tree, and helping it to establish quickly. Place the tree in the container.

4 BACKFILL, STAKE AND MULCH
Fill the gaps around the root ball with more compost and water well. Unless the tree already has a stake or cane, insert one now to hold the tree upright and to help anchor it in the pot. If it has a cane, carefully push it down into the new compost below. To conserve moisture and suppress weeds, apply a mulch of small pebbles or chipped bark.

Fruit trees are commonly grown on dwarf rootstocks, which limit the size of the tree. To grow fruit in containers, choose apples grown on M26, M9 or, for really small containers, M27. Look for pears grown on Quince C, cherries on Gisela 5, and for plums and damsons, choose those grown on Pixy.

5 WATERING AND FEEDING

It is essential to keep the fruit tree well watered, filling the pot to the brim each time. To encourage the best crop, don't allow it to dry out when in flower or fruit, and feed using a tomato fertilizer every two weeks during spring and summer. Although dormant, also water the tree during mild dry spells in late autumn and winter.

Train fruit trees

If you think your garden is too small for a fruit tree, you may be wrong. Fruit trees are some of the most amenable plants; they can be trained along walls and fences, taking up very little space, and look beautiful and even fruit better when grown in this way.

 WHEN TO START
Winter

AT ITS BEST
Spring and autumn

 TIME TO COMPLETE
🕐 5 hours

YOU WILL NEED

🖐 Several bare-root cordon apple
  or pear trees
  Bamboo canes
  Well-rotted organic matter, such
   as farmyard manure
  Spade
  Wires, vine eyes, and twine
  Mulch

1 MEASURE PLANTING DISTANCES
Fix horizontal wires to the fence or wall at 60cm (24in) intervals. Cordons can be planted as close together as 30cm (12in), depending on the effect you wish to create. Decide on your spacing, and measure along the wall or fence, marking each planting spot with a cane. Dig holes large enough to accommodate the root balls easily.

2 PLANT AND TRIM ROOTS
Plant the cordon at an angle of about 45° degrees. Examine the roots of each plant and cut off any that are large or woody, to encourage new feeding roots. Also, thin those that are above the soil. Ensure the graft union (scar on the stem) is above the surface.

3 ATTACH TREES TO CANES
Firm in the soil around the roots with your foot. Push the canes into the soil at the same angle as the trees. Tie the cordons to the canes, and tie the canes to the horizontal wires. Make sure all of your plants are securely fastened and aligned.

4 APPLY MULCH

Water the trees well after planting and apply a mulch of chipped bark, keeping clear of the stems, to retain moisture and suppress weeds. Water the trees regularly during their first year. Apply a tree and shrub granular fertilizer around the trees every spring, and replenish the mulch afterwards.

TOP TIP: ROUTINE PRUNING

Remove the flowers the first year after planting to encourage strong roots. Prune cordons each year in late summer. Shorten all woody sideshoots to within a few leaves of the stem to help promote fruiting spurs.

Make a home for frogs

Add a new dimension to a small garden or patio with a tiny pool made from a wooden barrel. Fill it with compact pond plants and soon you will find frogs, toads, water skaters, and other wildlife making their homes there too. The pool is best placed in a sunny spot that is in shade for part of the day.

WHEN TO START
Early spring

AT ITS BEST
Spring to late summer

TIME TO COMPLETE

 3 hours

YOU WILL NEED

Wooden half barrel
Strong plastic or butyl pond liner
Sharp knife or scissors
Galvanized nails and hammer
Aquatic pond baskets
Aquatic compost
Gravel and bricks

Marginal plants, those used
  here are:
Iris laevigata
Water forget-me-not, *Myosotis
  scorpioides* 'Alba'
Ragged robin, *Lychnis flos-cuculi*
Marsh marigold, *Caltha palustris*

1 LINE THE CONTAINER
Set the barrel where you intend to keep it because it will be very difficult to move once full of water. Place the pond liner over the top of the barrel, and push it down in the centre. Smooth it over the bottom and around the edges, pleating it neatly so that it lines the barrel evenly. Make sure that the liner reaches about 10cm (4in) above the rim at this stage.

2 ATTACH THE LINER
Fill the barrel with about 20cm (8in) of water and trim off excess liner just above the rim. With galvanized nails, shorter than the width of the wood, tack the liner to the barrel, then trim it above the nails.

3 FILL THE POOL
Fill the pool to about 10cm (4in) below the galvanized nails. Then plant up your pond plants. Add gravel to the top of each basket to prevent the soil from floating out.

4 ADD THE PLANTS
Check the label of each plant to see what depth it prefers. Most marginals like to grow with the tops of their baskets between 2–30cm (1–12in) below the water surface. To provide the correct depth, stand the plants on bricks in the barrel. The raised baskets also act like stepping stones, providing small creatures, such as frogs and toads, with easy access to and from the pool. To keep the water clear, include one or two oxygenating plants.

5 CREATE A WILDLIFE SANCTUARY
In spring, ask friends or neighbours with a pond for some frog or toad spawn, or tadpoles, to add to your barrel. Position other potted plants around the pool, so that the amphibians have landing places to hop in and out of the water. Snails and water insects will soon find their way to your pool too. From time to time, remove excess duckweed (small round leaves that float on the surface) with a net or old kitchen sieve, and take out algae using a stick.

Grow tasty bulbs

Onions, shallots, and garlic are among the most essential of all vegetables, adding strong, savoury flavours to a vast number of traditional and exotic dishes. Try out a range of cultivars for different tastes. Dry them well, and you can store the bulbs for use throughout winter.

Onions

Onions can be grown from seed or sets (small bulbs). Sets are more costly, and there is a smaller range of cultivars available, but they are quick, reliable, and a good choice for beginners.

 WHEN TO START
Early spring

AT THEIR BEST
Midsummer

 TIME TO COMPLETE

🕐 1 hour

YOU WILL NEED

 Onion sets
Spade
Horticultural grit for heavy soils
Rake
String line

1 PLANT SETS
Onions need good drainage, so add horticultural grit to heavier soils. Stretch a line of string between two pegs to make a straight row. Use a rake to form a shallow furrow, and plant the sets 15cm (6in) apart, with the tips protruding. Weed regularly, and water during dry spells.

2 LIFT AND DRY
Onions are ready for harvesting in midsummer, when the leaves turn yellow and fold over. Lift them and leave them in a cool, airy place to dry out for a couple of weeks. Use any with thick necks straightaway, and store the others for later.

Shallots

Many people prefer the sweet, milder flavour of shallots, as an alternative to onions. They can also be harvested earlier, and store longer than onions.

 WHEN TO START
Early spring

AT THEIR BEST
Mid-autumn

TIME TO COMPLETE

 1 hour

YOU WILL NEED

Shallot sets
Horticultural grit for heavy soil
String line
Rake

1 WHEN TO PLANT
In late winter or early spring, prepare the bed as for onions (*see left*). Plant shallots into well-drained soil, spacing them 15–20cm (6–8in) apart. Make a small hole, then push the shallot into the ground so that the top is just showing.

2 LIFT BULBS
Shallots form small clumps of bulbs, which you should lift intact. Dry and store them whole, somewhere dry and well ventilated, and break off individual bulbs as you need them. They will store well for up to 12 months.

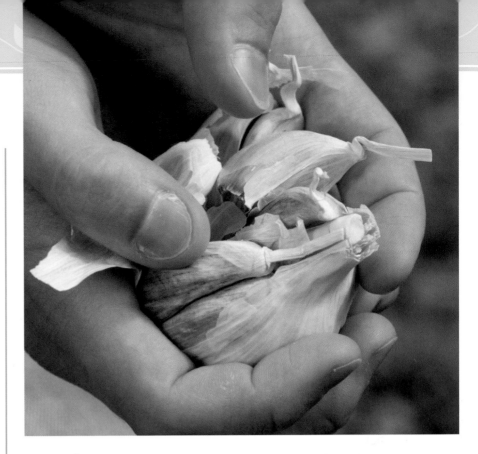

Garlic

Despite its reputation as an ingredient used in warmer countries, garlic is surprisingly easy to grow in cooler climes, although it needs a long growing season. Always use bulbs from a reputable supplier.

 WHEN TO START
Autumn

AT THEIR BEST
Summer

TIME TO COMPLETE

 1 hour

YOU WILL NEED

Garlic bulbs
Dibber
String line
Rake
Horticultural grit for
heavy soils

1 HOW TO PLANT
Plant into well-drained soil; add horticultural grit to heavy soils, or make and plant into a low ridge of soil. Split the bulb into individual cloves, plant with the point facing up, 10cm (4in) deep, 20cm (8in) apart, and cover with soil.

2 HARVEST AND DRY
Garlic is ripe when the leaves turn yellow in summer. Lift the bulbs and hang them to dry. Store individually or plait them together while the stems are dry but flexible. Starting with three bulbs, plait the stems until there is room to add more, then join the new stems to the other strings of the plait. Store in a cool, dry, well-ventilated place.

Create an easy-care border

This bold mix brings together rich colours and contrasting flowers and foliage to create an easy-care summer border. Ideal for free-draining soil and a sunny site, these plants rarely need watering once established.

⟩⟩ **WHEN TO START**
Early spring

AT ITS BEST
Summer

TIME TO COMPLETE
🕐 1 hour

YOU WILL NEED
💧 Horticultural grit
Well-rotted organic matter, such as farmyard manure
Spade
All-purpose granular fertilizer

1. Montbretia, *Crocosmia* 'Bressingham Blaze'

2. *Heliopsis helianthoides* Loraine Sunshine

3. *Lavandula angustifolia* Blue Cushion

4. *Sedum telephium* (Atropurpureum Group) 'Bressingham Purple'

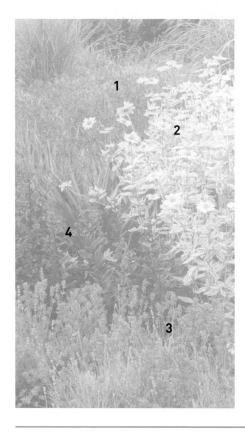

PREPARE THE SOIL
Choose a sunny, open position and, a week before planting, spread an 8cm (3in) layer of organic matter over the soil, and dig it into the top 15cm (6cm). Clay soils will also require horticultural grit to improve drainage.

PLANT THE PERENNIALS
Starting at the back of the border, plant the *Crocosmia*, with the *Heliopsis* and *Sedum* in front. Take care not to bury their stems, as this may cause them to rot.

PLANT THE LAVENDER
Plant a line of lavender at the front, ensuring that the stems are above the soil. Spread a gravel mulch. Water the plants regularly for the first year, until they are established. Apply a granular fertilizer each spring.

Easy-care shrubs

For a really low-maintenance border, try these hardy shrubs. They look after themselves once established, and tolerate periods of drought. Simply trim them annually to keep them in shape, removing dead, diseased or damaged stems.

❶ *Brachyglottis* (Dunedin Group) 'Sunshine' (evergreen, prefers sun); ↕1.5m (5ft) ↔2m (6ft) ❷ *Choisya* x *dewitteana* 'Aztec Pearl' (evergreen, prefers sun); ↕2.5m (8ft) ↔2.5m (8ft) ❸ *Mahonia* x *wagneri* cultivar (evergreen, prefers shade); ↕80cm (32in) ↔1m (3ft) ❹ *Viburnum sieboldii* (deciduous, prefers sun or partial shade); ↕4m (12ft) ↔4m (12ft)

Sow easy summer seeds

Growing summer bedding plants from seed is both fun and cost-effective, especially if you have several pots to fill. The seeds used in this scheme are French marigolds (*Tagetes*), *Bidens,* nasturtiums, and annual dahlias, all of which germinate quickly, and make a colourful display from summer until the first frosts.

Sow seed

Sow half-hardy seeds indoors in seed trays, but check the packets first for any specific instructions.

 WHEN TO START
Early spring

AT THEIR BEST
Summer

TIME TO COMPLETE

 A few hours over several weeks

YOU WILL NEED

 Packets of seed
Seed compost
Clean seed trays
Modular seed trays
Selection of pots
Broken clay pot pieces
Slow-release fertilizer
All-purpose compost
Watering can with rose

1 FILL SEED TRAYS
Using seed compost, fill some clean seed trays to within 2cm (1in) of the top. Gently press another seed tray on top to level out and firm the surface.

2 SOW SEEDS
Water the compost with a can fitted with a fine rose and allow to drain. Pour some seeds into your hand and carefully space them out on the compost surface. Sprinkle some sieved compost over the seeds, but check the packet first to see what depth the seeds require.

3 COVER AND KEEP MOIST
Label the seed tray, and put the lid, or a clear plastic bag, over the top. Place in a light spot, and check the packet to see what temperature the seeds need. Keep moist, and remove the lid or plastic bag as soon as seedlings emerge.

Large seeds

Large seeds, such as nasturtiums (*Tropaeolum*), can be planted in small 8cm (3in) pots, and will not need to be potted on (*see right*).

1 FILL POTS WITH COMPOST
Fill pots with seed compost and press it down gently with your fingers, or the bottom of another clean pot. Use a blunt pencil or dibber to make three holes, 2cm (1in) deep.

2 PLANT SEEDS
Drop one seed into each hole and press the compost down lightly. Label and water the pots, then place in a clear plastic bag until the seedlings start to emerge.

1 REMOVE SEEDLINGS FROM TRAY

Half-fill modular trays with good quality all-purpose compost. Holding the seedlings gently by their first leaves, use a pencil or dibber to gently tease their roots from the seed compost.

2 PLANT IN MODULES

Place a seedling in the middle of each cell of the modular tray, and fill around the roots and lower stems with more compost. Firm the compost using your fingertips to secure the seedlings.

3 WATER IN

Repeat Steps 1 and 2 for each seedling, and water carefully. Keep the seedlings in a bright place, and at the right temperature. A few weeks before the last frost is forecast, set them outside during the day, bringing them in at night, to harden them off.

Pot on seedlings

Check your seedlings daily and keep them well watered. The most effective way to do this is to place the seed trays in a larger container (with no drainage holes), half-filled with water. Leave them until the water has seeped into the compost and the surface is damp, then remove the seed trays. When the seedlings have a few leaves, pot them on as shown here.

Plant up the pots

In late spring when all frosts have finally finished, plant your bedding outside in pots, window boxes or hanging baskets. The plants raised here from six packets of seed filled five pots, three window boxes and a hanging basket. Choose containers that suit your garden design.

1 SATURATE CLAY POTS
Before planting up terracotta pots, soak them with water. Terracotta is porous, and saturating it first helps to prevent the clay from drawing moisture out of the compost when the pot is planted up.

2 ADD DRAINAGE MATERIAL
Place a layer of broken clay pot pieces in the base of each pot to ensure good drainage. To reduce the amount of compost needed for larger pots, fill the bottom third of the container with pieces of polystyrene (old plant trays are ideal).

3 APPLY FERTILIZER
Fill each container to about 5cm (2in) from the rim with all-purpose compost. Mix slow-release fertilizer designed for container plants into the compost. You can also add water-retaining gel crystals, which help to keep the compost moist, and reduce the need to water as frequently.

4 LIFT THE PLANTS
Water the young plants in their modules and leave to drain. Then gently squeeze the bottom and sides of each cell to loosen the root balls, and remove the plants. Place them on the compost about 10cm (4in) apart.

5 PLANT UP
In this scheme the dahlias are the tallest, and should be planted at the back, while the dwarf French marigolds need to be at the front, with the other plants dotted in–between. Plant up, firm the plants in gently, and water them well.

TOP TIP: AFTERCARE

Place the pots in a sunny position and water the plants regularly. Deadhead frequently to keep them in bloom for longer, removing faded flowers with secateurs. Young plants are prone to attacks by snails and slugs, so apply a few slug pellets, use nematodes or fix a copper band around the pots to keep them at bay. A gritty mulch may also help to deter pests. To retain moisture in the compost, you can add a decorative mulch, which will also help to set off the planting.

Pots of plenty >
Growing your own plants from seed is ideal if you have lots of pots to fill. The choice of varieties is also greater than the selection available as mature plants.

Foolproof seeds

Some annual seeds are almost infallible, and guaranteed to provide you with a garden full of bright, summer flowers. Protect half-hardy types from frost by planting them indoors in spring; others, such as pot marigolds, cornflowers, and love-in-a-mist, are hardy and can be sown directly into the soil or a container where they are to flower. That said, results are usually better if you start them off in pots indoors, and plant them out later.

✿✿✿ fully hardy   ✿✿ hardy in mild regions/sheltered sites   ✿ protect from frost over winter
☼ full sun   ☀ partial sun   ☀ full shade   ◇ well-drained soil   ◐ moist soil   ◆ wet soil

SELECTIONS

① Pot marigold, *Calendula officinalis*; ‡50cm (20in) ↔ 45cm (18in) ☼ ☀ ◇ ✿✿✿   **②** *Cosmos bipinnatus* 'Sonata White'; ‡1.5m (5ft) ↔ 45cm (18in) ☼ ◇ ◐ ✿   **③** Cornflower, *Centaurea cyanus*; ‡50cm (20in) ↔ 15cm (6in) ☼ ◇ ✿✿✿   **④** Tobacco plant, *Nicotiana* 'Lime Green'; ‡50cm (20in) ↔ 20cm (8in) ☼ ☀ ◐ ✿   **⑤** *Zinnia elegans* 'Peppermint Stick'; ‡60cm (24in) ↔ 40cm (16in) ☼ ◇ ✿   **⑥** Corn poppy, *Papaver rhoeas* Shirley Group; ‡90cm (36in) ↔ 30cm (12in) ☼ ◇ ✿✿✿   **⑦** Love-in-a mist, *Nigella damascena* Persian Jewel Series; ‡40cm (16in) ↔ 20cm (8in) ☼ ◇ ✿✿✿   **⑧** Love-lies-bleeding, *Amaranthus caudatus*; ‡1.2m (4ft) ↔ 60cm (24in) ☼ ◐ ✿   **⑨** *Callistephus chinensis* 'Pompon'; ‡60cm (24in) ↔ 45cm (18in) ☼ ◇ ◐ ✿   **⑩** California poppy, *Eschscholzia californica*; ‡30cm (12in) ↔ 15cm (6in) ☼ ◇ ✿✿✿

Wildlife wall

Many beneficial garden insects, such as ladybirds and ground beetles, struggle to find habitats in our neat gardens. Consider creating a wildlife wall to lure them in and keep them happy. It creates perfect homes for many different species, and its textures and patterns make it an attractive garden feature.

>> **WHEN TO MAKE**
Spring or summer

AT ITS BEST
Winter

TIME TO COMPLETE
 4 hours

YOU WILL NEED

Sedum or *Sempervivum* plants
Bricks (with holes in them)
Small blocks of wood, drilled
 with different sized holes
Roof tiles
Sheets of plywood or planks
 of wood
Straw, corrugated cardboard,
 slate chippings, bamboo canes,
 clumps of moss, twigs
Compost

1 CONSTRUCT THE WALL
In a quiet area of the garden, make a layer of bricks and tiles, leaving plenty of gaps. Place plywood or planks of wood on top and then add another layer of bricks and tiles. Top the structure off with the roof tiles, to keep excess moisture out.

2 STUFF THE GAPS
Cut the bamboo canes into short lengths and pack them into gaps to make homes for solitary bees. Roll up corrugated cardboard to create laying sites for ladybirds. Moss, slate chippings, straw and twigs pushed into the other holes will be colonized by many different garden insects. Plant the top with *Sedum* or *Sempervivum* to create a living roof.

3 AFTERCARE
Your wildlife wall, once built, should be left well alone; the more established (and decrepit) it becomes, the better it will be for wildlife, so don't be tempted to disturb it. However, you may need to occasionally top up some of the materials, particularly those such as straw that may be taken away as nest-building materials by birds.

Make a dead hedge

This is a simple way to make a wildlife-friendly corner from vines and twigs that cannot be composted. Small birds and insects will love it for shelter and food.

CONSTRUCTION TIPS
Use strong, long-lasting chestnut poles for the uprights, hammering them securely into the ground. For a neater look, use lengths of willow to weave loose sides. Then simply pile in shrub trimmings, lengths of ivy and bramble, and any other twigs the garden produces. Eventually, they will rot or compact down, and you can then add more to the top.

TOP TIP: CREATE A LOG HOME

A pile of old logs in the garden will attract beetles, frogs, toads, and other wildlife. Make a well-constructed pile, supported by a few posts hammered into the ground to prevent rolling. Leave the logs to rot down.

Turf a lawn

The quickest, if not cheapest, way to achieve a beautiful lawn is to lay turf, but if your money is to be well spent, take time to prepare your site a month or two beforehand.

TURF OPTIONS

Buy your turf from a specialist supplier, and if possible, inspect it before purchasing to ensure that it is weed- and disease-free. Reject turf with patches of yellow or dying grass. Your choice of turf will generally be limited to high-quality ornamental grass for formal lawns, and hardwearing utility turf for walkways and play areas.

Grass choices >
Price may be an issue, but good-quality turf from a reputable supplier may prove the best value for money in the long term.

Lay turf

Turf should not be stored for long, so agree a delivery date with your supplier that allows you to lay it immediately.

 WHEN TO START
Early autumn or early spring

AT ITS BEST
All year round

TIME TO COMPLETE
🕐 1 day to prepare; 1 day to lay turf

YOU WILL NEED
 Turf
Well-rotted organic matter, such as farmyard manure
Horticultural grit
All-purpose granular fertilizer
Rake and broom
Sharp knife
Top soil and horticultural sand

1 **PREPARE THE SITE**
Two months before the turf arrives, weed the site thoroughly. Dig 10cm (4in) of organic matter into the soil, and plenty of grit into heavy clay to increase drainage. Level with a rake. Tread over the soil on your heels in one direction, and repeat at right angles in the other direction.

2 **LAY THE FIRST ROW**
Remove stones and debris from the site, and leave for five weeks for the soil to settle. Weed the site again and apply an all-purpose granular fertilizer at the recommended rate. Make sure the soil is moist, not wet, before laying. Place the first piece of turf at one edge, and tamp it down with the back of a rake.

3 STAGGER THE JOINTS

Create a tight seam between turves by butting them together so they almost overlap and then pressing the crease down firmly with your thumbs. Continue to lay the turves in rows, and stagger the joints, like a brick wall. Stand on a plank of wood to protect the turf you have already laid.

4 APPLY A TOP DRESSING

Do not use small pieces at the edge of the lawn as they will dry out quickly and shrink – instead, lay them in the middle of the site. Scatter sandy loam, made from topsoil mixed with horticultural sand, into the joins and brush it into the turf to fill any gaps. Water well, and water the lawn in dry spells during the first growing season.

TOP TIP: SHAPING A LAWN

Use a hosepipe or rope to create a guide for a curved lawn, and with a half-moon grass cutter or sharp spade cut around your template. For a straight edge, stretch some string between two pegs pushed into the soil at each end.

Plant pots of perfume

The epitome of high summer, sweetly scented lilies set by a front or back door will greet you with their perfume as you come and go, but keep your distance as their pollen stains clothing. The most cost-effective way to grow them is to plant fresh bulbs in early spring.

 WHEN TO PLANT
Spring
AT THEIR BEST
Summer

TIME TO COMPLETE
🕐 30 minutes

YOU WILL NEED
🔧 Lily bulbs (*see Top Tip, right, for scented types*)
Deep container
Broken clay pot pieces
Multi-purpose compost
Horticultural grit

TOP TIP: LILY OPTIONS

Choose the following species for scent:

L. auratum
L. candidum
L. hansonii (below right)
L. regale, white
L. speciosum var. *rubrum* (below left)
Oriental hybrids, such as 'Star Gazer' (left), 'Tiger Woods', and 'Arabian Red'

1 PREPARE THE POT
In spring, buy fresh lily bulbs and choose a deep container; most lilies are planted at a depth of between 15–20cm (6–8in). Cover the drainage hole with broken pot pieces and then add a layer of multi-purpose compost.

2 PLANT THE BULBS
Add a 3cm (1½in) thick layer of horticultural grit over the compost and lay the bulbs on their sides on top. Positioning the bulbs like this allows water to drain out of the bulb scales, rather than collecting there and rotting the bulbs.

3 TOP UP THE CONTAINER
Cover the bulbs and top up the container to about 5cm (2in) below the rim with a 50:50 mix of compost and horticultural grit. Place your pots on "feet" in a sheltered spot and move them into the sun as soon as the shoots appear.

4 AFTERCARE
Water every couple of days, and apply a tomato feed to your lily pots every fortnight during the summer. Keep in a sheltered position over winter, and in spring, renew the top 5cm (2in) of compost. Lily beetle is their main pest. Look out for these bright red beetles and pick them off as soon as you see them.

Elegant arrangement

Clear white lilies with a frilly skirt of *Diascia* and dramatic striped grasses make a chic windowbox display for the front of the house. The lily used here is *Lilium* 'Reinesse', and like all Asiatic lilies it is unscented, but you could easily substitute a perfumed-type, such as 'Muscadet', to produce a fragrant combination.

1 PREPARE THE BOX

If your windowbox has no drainage holes, make a few with an electric drill. In early spring, add a layer of broken clay pot pieces to the bottom of the box, and cover them with compost. Plant up bulbs as shown opposite. Plant the delicate *Diascia* at the front of the box and the stripy *Carex* at each end. Or, for an instant effect in summer, buy the lilies in flower and pot them up with mature *Diascia* and *Carex* plants.

2 CARING FOR THE DISPLAY

Feed your windowbox every two weeks with a tomato fertilizer, and keep it well watered from late spring and throughout the summer. The lilies will flower for a few weeks in summer, and can then be planted out in the garden in free-draining soil. The *Diascia* will bloom continuously all summer and can survive the winter outside in mild areas; the *Carex* is quite hardy too, and is effective in winter displays.

TIME TO COMPLETE

 1 hour

YOU WILL NEED

Lilium 'Reinesse'
Diascia, white
Carex morrowii cultivar
Deep white windowbox
Broken clay pot pieces
Multi-purpose compost
Horticultural grit

TOP TIP: DEADHEADING DIASCIA

To help prolong the display, regularly remove fading flowers on your *Diascia*. This stops the plants producing seeds and focuses their energy on making more flowers instead.

Plant up productive pots

Although many vegetables need space to produce a worthwhile crop in a pot, there are plenty that can be grown successfully in more cramped conditions. Grow a container planted with vegetables outside your back door, and you can nip out and grab a handful whenever you need them.

Rainbow chard

Harvest these as colourful baby leaves, little and often, and use them in summer salads or stir-fries.

 WHEN TO PLANT
Spring to early summer

AT ITS BEST
Summer to autumn

TIME TO COMPLETE
🕐 30 minutes

YOU WILL NEED
 Small chard plants
Large, wide container
Broken clay pot pieces
Soil-based compost, such as
 John Innes No.3
Watering can

1 PREPARE CONTAINER
Make sure the container has adequate drainage holes and then cover the base with clay pot pieces. Top up the container with compost.

2 TEASE OUT ROOTS
Water small plants of rainbow or ruby chard. Tip them from their pots, and carefully tease out the roots. This helps them establish quickly.

3 PLANT AND FIRM IN
Plant the chard fairly close together for a good display. Firm in and water well. Keep well watered and cut back flowering stems to prolong the crop.

Radishes

Radishes are great crops for containers. They are the fastest germinating and maturing vegetable of all, grow almost anywhere, and their peppery taste gives salads a real kick.

 WHEN TO PLANT
Spring to summer

AT ITS BEST
Late spring to early autumn

TIME TO COMPLETE

🕐 30 minutes

YOU WILL NEED

💧 Radish seed
Low, wide pot
Broken clay pot pieces
Soil-based compost, such as
 John Innes No.3
Watering can with fine rose

1 PREPARE AND SOW
Cover the base of the pot with broken pot pieces. Fill the container with compost and firm the top lightly. Sow seed on the surface and cover with 1cm (½in) of compost. Water with a fine rose.

2 THIN OUT
As seedlings germinate and grow, thin them out, leaving the others to mature fully. You can eat the removed seedlings as an extra early salad crop.

3 HARVEST
Water your pot regularly. Radishes are usually ready about five weeks after sowing. Do not allow them to grow for longer than this, as their taste becomes hotter and unpleasant, and they lose their crunch. To harvest, simply pull them up when ready. They store well in the fridge for a few days.

TOP TIP: BABY BEANS FOR CONTAINERS

'Hestia' is one of the smallest runner beans. Being compact, with beautiful flowers, it is well suited to growing in pots. Dwarf runner beans do not climb and need minimal support – just a few short canes to hold them up in windy weather. Prepare the pot as for radishes. Grow one plant per pot, and water them frequently. Pick regularly once the beans start appearing to prolong the harvest.

Pot up delicious strawberries

Growing strawberries in containers suits them perfectly because it lifts the fruits off the ground, keeping them away from slugs, mice, and other pests, as well as wet soil that can cause the berries to rot. Replace your strawberries with fresh, young plants every few years.

 WHEN TO PLANT
Early spring

AT THEIR BEST
Summer

TIME TO COMPLETE

🕐 1½ hours

YOU WILL NEED

 Three strawberry plants
Large pot
Broken clay pot pieces
Multi-purpose compost
Slow-release granular fertilizer
Bark chips
Straw

1 PREPARE TO PLANT
Take three young, healthy plants and water them thoroughly, an hour before planting. Cover the holes in the base of the large pot with broken clay pieces to prevent compost from blocking them, and then add compost until the pot is two-thirds full. Firm down lightly.

2 EASE PLANTS FROM SMALL CONTAINERS

Take the plants out of their pots and check the roots. If they are root bound, and running in tight circles inside the pot, tease them out carefully to help the plants establish quicker.

3 PLANT AROUND EDGE OF POT

Place the three plants around the edges of the pot so that the fruits will dangle over. Fill all around them with compost, add some fertilizer granules and then firm down. Water well, and daily thereafter.

4 REMOVE FLOWERS

You will have healthier plants in the long run if you sacrifice the first year's fruits, allowing them to concentrate on root growth. Nip out the flowers as they appear. The following year, apply a tomato fertilizer every week after the flower buds form.

TOP TIP: PROTECTING THE FRUITS

Strawberry fruits can rot if they come into contact with wet soil. While most grown in a pot will hang over the sides, avoid any problems by placing a straw mulch around the top of the pot to lift fruits away from the compost.

Tip-top berries

Strawberries can also be grown in hanging baskets or windowboxes. Dainty, tasty alpines are the best choice for this type of container.

 WHEN TO PLANT
Early spring

AT THEIR BEST
Summer

TIME TO COMPLETE
🕐 1½ hours

YOU WILL NEED

 Alpine strawberry plants
Hanging basket or windowbox
Multi-purpose compost
Slow-release granular fertilizer

1 PLANT THE WINDOWBOX

Plant small plants fairly close together to give an impressive show, and a good harvest. Add some slow-release fertilizer granules to the compost as you plant, and keep the plants well watered throughout the year.

2 HARVESTING AND CARE

Harvest and eat the berries as they ripen throughout summer. Check the plants frequently and pick regularly to encourage later fruits to ripen. The plants will need lifting out of the pot and dividing every three or four years.

Flowers for cutting and drying

One of the greatest pleasures of owning a garden is growing an abundance of flowers, many of which can be picked and brought indoors to decorate the house as well. Some are particularly well suited to cutting, while others can be harvested and dried to last into winter and beyond.

Cutting

Many plants can be cut frequently with little impact on the garden display; they just keep on producing more flowers. Plant a cut-flower border full of such varieties.

Allium	Dahlia
Alstroemeria	Foxglove, *Digitalis*
Antirrhinum	Peony (*above*)
Chrysanthemum	*Rudbeckia*
Cleome	Sunflower
Cornflower,	Sweet pea
Centaurea	Sweet William
Cosmos	Tulip
Daffodil	*Zinnia*

 WHEN TO START
Autumn or spring

AT THEIR BEST
Spring to late summer

TIME TO COMPLETE

 5 hours for sowing and pricking out
2 hours for planting

YOU WILL NEED

 Seeds of annuals
Bulbs
Perennials
Spade
Well-rotted organic matter, such
 as farmyard manure
Watering can

1 PLANT IN SWATHES
Clear the area of weeds, and dig in organic matter. In autumn, plant bulbs and mark their positions. Then, in spring, plant large swathes of perennials and annuals (*see pp.24–25*), so that you can cut the flowers regularly without leaving large gaps in your border.

2 PICK AND MIX
When you are planning to pick your flowers, water the area well the night before. This helps the stems to plump up, and the cut flowers will keep for longer. It is best to cut first thing in the morning, plunging the stems immediately into a deep bucket of water. Always cut to just above a leaf.

Drying

Some flowers retain their colours and scents when they are cut and dried, and can be used in flower arrangements throughout the year. Seedheads look striking in indoor arrangements too, but leave some on the plants if you want a dramatic winter border.

WHEN TO START
Summer to autumn

AT THEIR BEST
All year

TIME TO COMPLETE
About 2 weeks for drying

YOU WILL NEED
Flowers for drying
Rubber bands
Tacks or pins
Hooks or paperclips
String

1 PLANT AND SOW

Several perennials are useful as dried flowers, but you may want to sow some annuals too. Sow half-hardy annuals into modules or pots indoors in spring, planting out when all risk of frost has passed (*see pp.24–25*). Hardy annuals can be sown direct in autumn or spring. Water, feed, and deadhead as you would any other plant.

2 CUT IN DRY WEATHER

Pick flowers for drying in fine weather to avoid excess moisture on the foliage and petals. Most flowers will dry better if they are cut before they are fully open. Pick roses just as the buds begin to open, and lavender stems as the top petals start to emerge.

3 AIR DRY THE BLOOMS

Tie a few stems together with a rubber band or string. Use a kitchen hook or a paper clip to attach the bands to a line of string, or tie them to a bamboo cane (*below*). Then fix the string or cane to the ceiling in a cool, airy place. As strong light will bleach out the colours, it is best to hang them in the dark, or in low light.

FLOWERS FOR DRYING

Achillea (above)
Cornflower,
  Centaurea
Globe thistle,
  Echinops
Hare's tail,
  Lagurus
Lavender
Love-in-a-mist,
  Nigella

Quaking grass,
  Briza
Sea holly,
  Eryngium
Statice,
  Limonium
  (above)
Strawflower,
  Xerochrysum
  (below)

Plant dahlia tubers

Once shunned by fashionable gardeners, these flashy, colourful jewels have staged something of a comeback, and are now considered an essential feature of the mid- to late-summer border, as well as injecting life into tired autumn gardens. They also provide lots of cut flowers for indoor displays.

 WHEN TO PLANT
Late spring

AT THEIR BEST
Midsummer to autumn

TIME TO COMPLETE

🕐 30 minutes for planting

YOU WILL NEED

● Dahlia tubers
Well-rotted organic matter, such as farmyard manure
Slug rings or organic pellets
Canes and twine for staking
Wooden boxes
Potting compost
Plant labels

1 PLANT THE TUBERS
Just before the danger of frost has passed, dig a hole 30cm (12in) deep and add a layer of organic matter to the bottom. Place the tuber in with the buds pointing up, as well as a cane for support, and carefully refill with soil.

2 PINCH OUT SHOOT TIPS
Provide slug protection as young growth appears. When the stems are 30cm (12in) high, pinch out the top bud to encourage bushiness and lots of flowers.

3 FROST PROTECTION
As soon as the first light frost has blackened the leaves, cut off the foliage and dig up the tubers. Place them somewhere airy and frost free, so that the stems can dry out fully.

4 STORE OVERWINTER
When dry, brush the soil off the tubers, label them clearly and plant them in wooden boxes or large pots of dry potting compost. Keep them in a cool, dry, frost-free place until you can plant them out again the following spring.

Try tropical cannas

Cannas bring tropical colour to the late-summer garden, but are not entirely hardy. They are tougher than dahlias, though, and can survive outside in milder areas with the right care.

>> **WHEN TO PLANT**
Late spring

AT THEIR BEST
Midsummer to autumn

TIME TO COMPLETE
🕐 30 minutes for planting

YOU WILL NEED
🌱 Canna rhizomes
Well-rotted organic matter, such as farmyard manure
Mulch
Straw
Chicken wire or wooden box

1 SITING CANNAS
These plants need a hot and sunny spot to flower well; a south-facing, sheltered area is ideal. Also, make sure that your cannas are not shaded by neighbouring plants, or competing with them for moisture, which can affect flowering.

2 IMPROVE THE SOIL
Cannas are thirsty plants, so improve the soil with organic matter to help retain moisture. To plant, dig a hole about 20cm (8in) deep and lay a rhizome in it horizontally. Refill the hole with soil, water well, and apply a layer of mulch.

3 OVERWINTERING
In autumn, after the frost has blackened the leaves, cut down the stems. In mild regions, cover the rhizomes with straw, pinned down with chicken wire. In colder areas, lift and store them in dry potting compost, in a cool, dry, frost-free place, such as a shed.

SELECTIONS >>

Dramatic dahlias

The darlings of the gardening design world, dahlias are the glamour pusses of the mid- to late-summer border, providing sparkle and drama just as other stars are starting to fade. Choose from simple singles, neat pompons, star-shaped cactus-types, and dainty collerettes in a wide range of rich colours. Use them to colour up beds and borders, or to create eye-catching displays in large containers on a patio or terrace.

❀❀❀ fully hardy   ❀❀ hardy in mild regions/sheltered sites   ❀ protect from frost over winter
☼ full sun   ☀ partial sun   ● full shade   ◌ well-drained soil   ◖ moist soil   ● wet soil

① 'Gay Princess'; ↕1.5m (5ft) ↔75cm (30in) ☼ ◌ ❀   **②** 'Arabian Night'; ↕1.2m (4ft) ↔ 60cm (24in) ☼ ◌ ❀   **③** 'Easter Sunday'; ↕1m (3ft) ↔ 60cm (24in) ☼ ◌ ❀   **④** 'Kathryn's Cupid'; ↕1.2m (4ft) ↔ 60cm (24in) ☼ ◌ ❀   **⑤** 'Ragged Robin'; ↕1m (3ft) ↔ 45cm (18in) ☼ ◌ ❀   **⑥** 'Yellow Hammer'; ↕60cm (24in) ↔ 45cm (18in) ☼ ◌ ❀   **⑦** 'Preston Park'; ↕45cm (18in) ↔ 45cm (18in) ☼ ◌ ❀   **⑧** 'Moonfire'; ↕1m (3ft) ↔ 60cm (24in) ☼ ◌ ❀   **⑨** 'Pink Giraffe'; ↕75cm (30in) ↔ 60cm (24in) ☼ ◌ ❀   **⑩** 'Polar Sight'; ↕1.2m (4ft) ↔ 60cm (24in) ☼ ◌ ❀   **⑪** 'Zorro'; ↕1.2m (4ft) ↔ 60cm (24in) ☼ ◌ ❀

《SELECTIONS》

Cottage dream

The gentle hues and varying textures of cottage garden perennials can be used to create beautiful combinations in an informal planting scheme. This is the classic sun-loving border of many gardeners' imaginations, with spires of lofty delphiniums piercing through lower mounds of colourful flowers.

≫ **WHEN TO START**
Autumn

AT THEIR BEST
Midsummer

TIME TO COMPLETE
🕐 2 hours preparation; 3 hours to plant

YOU WILL NEED
Spade
Well-rotted organic matter
Grit

1. *Delphinium* Black Knight Group
2. *Anchusa azurea*
3. *Alstroemeria ligtu* hybrids
4. *Achillea filipendulina* 'Gold Plate'
5. *Salvia sclarea* var. *turkestanica*
6. *Verbascum olympicum*

1 PREPARE THE SOIL
In autumn, clear the border of all weeds. Dig in organic matter, such as garden compost or well-rotted farmyard manure. Ideally you should dig down one spade depth, incorporating organic matter into the top 15cm (6in) of soil. On heavy soils, spread a layer of grit over the whole area, and dig it in to improve drainage.

2 SET OUT THE PLANTING PLAN
Buy plants in spring and set them out across the border, taking time to arrange them and to visualize how they will grow in relation to each other. The classic arrangement is taller plants at the back and shorter plants at the front, but consider using tall, airy types, such as *Achillea* or *Verbena bonariensis*, further forward.

3 AFTERCARE
Some of the plants will need staking as they grow (*see right*), and in their first year they will require regular watering to help them to establish. Although these herbaceous perennials die back in winter, where possible, leave their stems to stand until spring. Then cut everything back to the ground to tidy the border and allow space for new growth. This is also a good time to apply a general-purpose granular fertilizer and a mulch of well-rotted organic matter.

TOP TIP: STAKING

Many perennials, such as delphiniums and *Achillea*, become top-heavy and require support. If you provide supports early in the season, plants will grow through and disguise them, and they will still look natural and attractive. Plants staked at a later date, once they have already flopped, always tend to look trussed up.

∧ *Stop the flop*
Use short canes to support tall flowers, such as delphiniums (top left). *Plants with mound-like growth will grow through and be supported by twiggy sticks put in place in spring* (top right). *Linked metal stakes serve a similar purpose* (above).

SELECTIONS >>

Cottage garden plants

There are so many different plants that suit a cottage garden, but as a rule, the simpler ones that have not been highly bred look most at home in such a scheme. Plants such as anemones, *Cirsium* and *Anthemis* create easy-going, loose arrangements, while the tall flower spires of lupins and hollyhocks provide structure. Cottage garden plants are generally loved by bees and other nectar-seeking insects.

❋❋❋ fully hardy　❋❋ hardy in mild regions/sheltered sites　❋ protect from frost over winter

☼ full sun　◐ partial sun　● full shade　◊ well-drained soil　◗ moist soil　● wet soil

❶ Monkshood, *Aconitum carmichaelii* Arendsii Group; ‡1.2m (4ft) ↔30cm (12in) ☼ ◐ ◊ ◗ ❋❋❋

❷ Golden marguerite, *Anthemis tinctoria* 'E.C. Buxton'; ‡60cm (24in) ↔90cm (36in) ☼ ◊ ❋❋❋

❸ *Aquilegia formosa*; ‡60cm (24in) ↔45cm (18in) ☼ ◐ ◗ ❋❋❋　**❹** *Coreopsis verticillata* 'Moonbeam'; ‡50cm (20in) ↔60cm (24in) ☼ ◐ ◊ ◗ ❋❋❋　**❺** *Cirsium rivulare* 'Atropurpureum'; ‡1.2m (4ft) ↔60cm (24in) ☼ ◊ ◗ ❋❋❋　**❻** Bleeding heart, *Dicentra spectabilis* 'Alba'; ‡1.2m (4ft) ↔45cm (18in) ◐ ◗ ❋❋❋　**❼** *Anemone hupehensis* 'Hadspen Abundance'; ‡60cm (24in) ↔40cm (16in) ☼ ◐ ◗ ❋❋❋　**❽** Meadow cranesbill, *Geranium pratense* 'Mrs Kendall Clark'; ‡60cm (24in) ↔60cm (24in) ☼ ◐ ◊ ◗ ❋❋❋　**❾** Lupin, *Lupinus* 'Inverewe Red'; ‡90cm (36in) ↔60cm (24in) ☼ ◐ ◊ ❋❋❋　**❿** Hollyhock, *Alcea rosea* Chater's Double Group; ‡2.4m (8ft) ↔60cm (24in) ☼ ◊ ❋❋❋　**⓫** *Astrantia major*; ‡60cm (24in) ↔45cm (18in) ☼ ◐ ◗ ❋❋❋

Grow plants from plugs

Quick, easy and cheap, "plugs" are basically well-developed seedlings that you pot on once before planting out. They are ideal if you do not have the space or time to sow seeds yourself, and they are the simplest option for plants that are difficult to germinate. Mail-order companies tend to offer the largest selection of bedding and tender perennial plugs, and they usually cost a fraction of the price of fully-grown plants.

 WHEN TO START
Spring
AT THEIR BEST
Late spring to autumn

TIME TO COMPLETE
 1½ hours

YOU WILL NEED
Plug plants – begonias have been used here
Dibber or pencil
Potting compost
Large modular trays or small 8cm (3cm) plastic pots
Watering can

1 ORDER YOUR PLUGS
When ordering plugs, make sure you will have time to pot them up soon after they arrive – most companies specify when they will be delivered. Plugs are also known as "miniplants" or "easiplants", and companies may offer them at different stages of development. The youngest plugs will be cheapest.

2 REMOVE PLUGS FROM CONTAINER
When the plugs arrive, water well and store them in a cool, frost-free place. Fill large modular trays, or small 8cm (3in) pots, with good-quality potting compost, designed for seedlings and young plants. Using the blunt end of a pencil or a dibber, gently push the plug plants out of their original containers.

3 PLANT UP IN MODULES
Make a hole with your finger or a pencil in the compost in the modules, and insert a plug plant in each. Firm the compost around the plug lightly with your fingers, taking care not to compact it or to damage the roots.

4 KEEP PLANTS WATERED
Water the plugs using a can fitted with a fine rose, and keep them in a cool, light, frost-free place. Water regularly, harden off (see p.25), and plant out in pots, or in the ground, when all risk of frost has passed.

Planting options

Most popular bedding plants, including pelargoniums, busy Lizzies, begonias, lobelia, snapdragons, dahlias and fuchsias are available as plug plants, although many companies also offer a selection of newer and more unusual varieties. Order in early spring for a late spring delivery.

❶ *Nicotiana* 'Nicki'; ↕45cm (18in)
❷ *Nemesia strumosa* 'KLM'; ↕25cm (10in)
❸ *Gazania* Chansonette Series; ↕30cm (12in)
❹ *Pelargonium* Horizon Series; ↕40cm (16in)

< *Shady treat*
This beautiful container, ideal for a partly shaded spot, is filled with Begonia 'Illumination Rose' and fragrant blue heliotropes, all grown from plugs, together with Fuchsia 'Genii' and trailing Lysimachia nummularia 'Aurea' (golden creeping Jenny).

Make cottage-style containers

Even if you don't own a traditional garden with deep borders, you can still pull off the cottage garden look by planting in containers. Herbaceous perennials and annual climbers grow well in pots, which you can slot into existing planting schemes to add extra height and colour wherever you want it.

Morning glory tower

This annual climber, *Ipomoea*, can be easily grown from seed in spring, and will quickly romp over a container support, smothering it in trumpet-like flowers.

 WHEN TO START
Spring

AT ITS BEST
Mid- to late summer

TIME TO COMPLETE
2 hours

YOU WILL NEED

Morning glory, *Ipomoea*, seedlings
Large container
Multi-purpose compost and
 slow-release fertilizer
Broken clay pot pieces
Tall bamboo canes
Raffia or string

1 BEFORE YOU PLANT
Place broken clay pot pieces in the base of the pot, fill with compost, and mix in slow-release fertilizer granules.

2 TIE CANES TOGETHER
Arrange the canes around the edge of the pot and tie the tops together. Then stabilize the obelisk by tying each cane to the next with raffia to form a ring. Repeat this a few times up the canes.

3 PLANT SEEDLINGS
Take a pot or two of seedlings that you sowed indoors (*see pp.24–25*) in early spring. Carefully separate them out and plant one at the base of each cane. Firm in, and water the plants well.

4 AFTERCARE
The small plants will quickly start to climb of their own accord but may benefit from being tied in at first. Water the plants well all summer, and remove any spent flowers to keep them in bloom.

Pastel pot

Compact versions of cottage garden perennials grow well in pots, where they make a looser and more natural alternative to tender bedding plants.

 WHEN TO START
Spring

AT ITS BEST
Summer

TIME TO COMPLETE

 1 hour

YOU WILL NEED

Wide pot
Broken clay pot pieces
Soil-based compost, such as
 John Innes No.3
Slow-release fertilizer granules

Carex 'Ice Dance'
Delphinium grandiflorum
Stachys officinalis 'Hummelo'
Veronica spicata 'Rosenrot'

1 PREPARE AND PLANT
Place broken clay pot pieces over the holes in the base of the container, then half-fill it with compost. Plant the delphinium towards the back and arrange the other, lower-growing plants in front. Fill around them with more compost, and mix in slow-release fertilizer granules. Water the plants well.

2 AFTERCARE
With the correct care, this can be a long-lasting container that flowers year after year. In early spring, remove all dead growth to make way for the new spring shoots. At the same time, remove the top layer of compost, and replace with fresh compost mixed with fertilizer granules. The plants will also require regular division (*see right*).

TOP TIP: REPOTTING AND DIVIDING PERENNIALS

In the garden, herbaceous perennials need lifting, dividing and replanting every few years to keep them healthy. In a pot, this should be done more often, at least every two years. Lift the plants out of the pot and use your hands to tease sections apart. Discard any old or weak clumps, then replant the healthiest offsets into fresh compost with some fertilizer.

Create a lavender hedge

The perfume from a lavender hedge is without equal, while the beautiful purple flowers attract scores of bees and butterflies in summer. The strongest scent is released when the flowers are brushed, so plant your hedge where you can run your fingers through the stems as you pass.

WHEN TO PLANT
Spring

AT ITS BEST
Summer

TIME TO COMPLETE

 2 hours

YOU WILL NEED

Small lavender plants
Well-rotted organic matter, such as
 farmyard manure
Horticultural grit
Trowel or small spade
All-purpose liquid fertilizer

1 PREPARE THE GROUND
A month or two before planting your hedge, dig plenty of well-rotted organic matter into the soil to improve drainage. Also dig horticultural grit into heavy clay soils, as lavender will rot in wet conditions.

SPACE PLANTS EVENLY
2 In spring, buy small plants and make holes at 30cm (12in) intervals, or dig out a long trench. The plants will not require additional fertilizer at this stage. Plant the lavenders so they are at the same level as they were in their pots.

FIRM IN SOIL
3 In heavier, clay-rich soil, plant the lavenders slightly above the soil surface, and draw up soil around the root ball, to encourage water to drain away from the base of the plant. Firm in around all the plants with your fingers.

WATER IN
4 Water the plants well. Although lavenders are very drought-tolerant, they will need to be watered for the first growing season until they are fully established. In spring, apply an all-purpose liquid fertilizer to the plants and cut them back twice a year (*see right*).

Shear your lavender

Although lavenders are generally easy plants, requiring little or no additional watering once established, they do need annual care. Leave small, young plants unpruned for the first 12 months after planting to allow them to put on some growth, but in subsequent years cut your hedge twice a year to prevent it becoming leggy.

》 **WHEN TO START**
Late summer, after flowering, and early spring

TIME TO COMPLETE
1 hour or longer depending on hedge size

YOU WILL NEED
Garden shears
Household disinfectant
Secateurs
All-purpose liquid fertilizer

PRUNE INTO SHAPE
1 To keep your lavender plants young, bushy and healthy, cut them back in late winter or early spring. Clean your tools thoroughly and spray them with a household disinfectant before you begin work. Then, using sharp shears, cut the stems back as close as possible to the old wood.

THE CORRECT CUT
2 Take care not to cut into old brown wood, since the plants will not reshoot from this. Shear to a few healthy leaves above the brown stems (*right*), and work systematically along the hedge, keeping it as level as possible.

AFTER FLOWERING
3 In late spring or early summer, the sheared plants will grow an abundance of side shoots to create a compact, bushy hedge. To keep it neat, cut it back again after flowering in late summer: remove all the old flowerheads to prevent the plants putting their energy into making unwanted seed.

Make a wall of fiery geraniums

Wander down any residential street in the Mediterranean region and you will find houses ablaze with fiery geraniums. These drought-loving plants bask happily in the burning sun in their tiny terracotta pots, creating a dazzling display that requires very little care. If you have a sunny wall, buy young plants in late spring to create your own summer holiday effect at home.

WHEN TO PLANT
Late spring

AT THEIR BEST
Early summer to early autumn

 TIME TO COMPLETE
2 hours

YOU WILL NEED

- Bedding geraniums, *Pelargonium*
Small terracotta wall pots
Broken clay pot pieces and gravel
Multi-purpose compost
Slow-release all-purpose fertilizer
Masonry nails or Rawlplugs
 and coach bolts
Hammer or electric drill

1 PREPARE THE WALL POTS

Buy at least five wall pots and make sure that each has a drainage hole – if not, make one with an electric drill. Cover the hole with a piece of clay pot. Add 2cm (1in) of gravel and then a layer of compost to the base of each container.

2 PLANT THE GERANIUMS

Water the plants. Put one geranium (*Pelargonium*), still in its original container, into the wall pot and check that it will sit at least 2cm (1in) below the rim when planted. Remove it from its pot and plant up, firming in around it with multi-purpose compost mixed with a little slow-release fertilizer. Water well.

3 FIX POTS TO WALL

For a more dramatic effect, paint the wall white or a pale colour. Hammer in a masonry nail at a slight angle; alternatively, if you can't drive in a nail, drill a hole with an electric drill, push in a Rawlplug, and screw in a coach bolt. Fit the pots on to the wall.

TOP TIP: WATERING YOUR POTS

Geraniums require watering every few days in summer, so make sure you can reach them easily or use a long-handled hose. As the plants grow and their roots develop, it is best to water them from below by placing the wall pots in a bowl of water for 30 minutes.

< *Colourful combinations*
Choose either a single colour theme, or try geraniums in a combination of matching shades, as shown here.

Build a timber raised bed

If you have a heavy clay soil, you may find it easier to grow your vegetables in raised beds, which offer many advantages. Not only does the soil drain freely, making them ideal for root crops, but it also warms up more quickly in spring, allowing you to sow and plant sooner, and enjoy earlier harvests.

WHEN TO START
Winter

AT ITS BEST
Summer

TIME TO COMPLETE

1 day

YOU WILL NEED

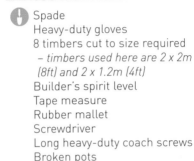

Spade
Heavy-duty gloves
8 timbers cut to size required
 – *timbers used here are 2 x 2m
 (8ft) and 2 x 1.2m (4ft)*
Builder's spirit level
Tape measure
Rubber mallet
Screwdriver
Long heavy-duty coach screws
Broken pots
Top soil or soil-based compost,
 such as John Innes No.3

1 DIG OUT STRIPS OF TURF
Mark out lines on the ground where the timbers will rest, then use a sharp spade to cut out the outline of your bed, all the way around. If positioning the bed on a lawned area, ease the spade between turf and soil, and lift off the grass, which you can then use elsewhere in the garden.

2 LAY TIMBERS IN POSITION
Set the first layer of timbers in position. Remove or add soil until they are level. Check the levels along and diagonally across the timbers with a builder's spirit level. Ensure the base is square by checking that the diagonals are equal in length. For a perfect square or rectangle, have the timbers pre-cut at a timber yard.

3 SECURE BASE TIMBERS
Use a rubber mallet to adjust the position of the timbers so they butt up and align neatly at the corners. Drill two holes on one side of each corner, and secure the joint using long, heavy-duty coach screws. Check that all timbers are firmly joined together.

4 ARRANGE SECOND LAYER
The next layer of timbers simply sit on top of the first. Arrange the pieces so that the joints at the four corners are staggered, as shown, to give the structure extra strength and stability. Check all levels before screwing the timbers in place, as shown in Step 3.

5 SOW SEEDS OR PLANT PLUGS
For added drainage, put a layer of broken pots or builder's rubble in the base, then fill with garden topsoil or soil-based compost, such as John Innes No.3. Water it well and leave to settle for a few days, after which you can sow seeds or plant directly.

< *Convenience food*
Position a raised bed near your patio and you can have fresh salad leaves and herbs close to the kitchen and barbecue area.

Roots for raised beds

Root vegetables, such as carrots and beetroot, commonly produce misshapen roots if they are grown in stony garden soil. Since these, and most other root crops, also prefer a free-draining soil, they are ideal for growing in raised beds, where their tasty, succulent roots can develop straight and true.

 WHEN TO START
Spring
AT THEIR BEST
Summer, autumn, and winter

 TIME TO COMPLETE
1½ hours

 YOU WILL NEED
Seed for root vegetables, such as carrot, radish, beetroot, and celeriac

Beetroot

Reliable and easy to grow, beetroot comes in yellow, white, and striped varieties, as well as the traditional blood-red. Sow a new batch every few weeks and harvest the plump, sweet, earthy roots as you need them.

1 SOWING
Sow seeds 1.5cm (¾in) deep in rows, directly in the soil, every two weeks from late spring. Thin the seedlings shortly after germination so plants are 15cm (6in) apart.

2 HARVESTING
Beetroot is sweetest and most succulent when young, and can be harvested when roots reach the size of a golf ball. Leave some in the ground to grow larger, where they will last into winter. Pull them as required, although they will eventually become tougher and less tasty. When you harvest the beetroot, cut leaves bleed and stain; instead, simply twist off the leafy tops.

Celeriac

The edible part of celeriac is actually the swollen base of the stem, not the root. Since this develops below soil level, it is commonly regarded as a root vegetable.

1 SOWING AND PLANTING

In early spring, sow seed in modules in a greenhouse or cold frame. Germination can be slow, and the plants need a long season to mature fully. Pot them on as they grow. When they are about 7cm (3in) tall, harden them off outside (*see p.25*). Then plant them out into well-drained soil, at a distance of about 15cm (6in) apart.

2 HARVESTING

Celeriac can be harvested from late summer and throughout winter. As they do not store well once dug up, leave them in the soil until you need them. Cold weather improves the flavour of celeriac but can damage the plants. A mulch of straw applied before the first frosts will prevent this and keep your crop in a good condition until you harvest it.

Carrots

Carrots are the mainstay of the allotment and kitchen, but they are slightly fussy, and need really free-draining soil to do well. They are also prone to a troublesome pest, carrot fly larvae, which you need to guard against.

1 SOWING IN DRILLS

Sow seeds 1.5cm (¾in) deep directly into the soil from mid-spring. As they grow you can thin them out and eat as baby carrots, leaving the others in the ground to mature. Try not to bruise their leaves when pulling them out, as the smell attracts carrot fly (*see Top Tip, below*).

2 HARVESTING

Carrots are ready to harvest from midsummer. On sandy soils, you can simply pull them out of the ground, but on heavier soils use a fork, taking care not to damage the roots. Harvest young carrots to use immediately. Older ones can be stored in a cool place over winter.

TOP TIP: PROTECTIVE COVERING

The carrot fly locates carrots by scent, and then lays eggs nearby. As these hatch, the larvae burrow into the necks of the roots, at the base of the foliage, often making the carrots inedible. To prevent this, simply cover the crop with a light, transparent mesh, such as garden fleece, dug into the soil at the bottom. Alternatively, surround your crop with a solid barrier 75cm (30in) high, as the adults can only fly close to the ground.

Winter pickings

Winter can be a surprisingly bountiful time on the vegetable plot, but you need to plan ahead carefully for a good crop of vegetables. Start sowing the previous spring, giving your plants all summer and autumn to bulk up, and you should have plenty of fresh produce for winter dishes.

Leeks

Grow leeks as part of a crop rotation, as they will quickly succumb to diseases if replanted in the same spot year after year. Planting them deep produces white and tender stems.

››› **WHEN TO START**
Spring

AT THEIR BEST
Winter

TIME TO COMPLETE
 30 minutes for sowing
1½ hours for planting out

YOU WILL NEED
 Leek seed
Seed tray
Seed compost
Dibber or slim trowel

1 SOW IN TRAYS
In spring, sow seed thinly across a seed tray and keep in a cold frame or cool, sheltered spot while they germinate. When the seedlings are about 20cm (8in) tall, they are ready for planting out.

2 PLANT OUT
In a well-prepared bed, mark out a line and use your dibber to make holes 20cm (8in) deep and 15cm (6in) apart. Drop a leek into each hole, making sure the roots reach the bottom, and then water them in. There is no need to backfill with soil; this will happen slowly, of its own accord, allowing some light to reach the small leek plants.

3 CROP CARE AND HARVEST
Leeks require very little attention after planting. You only need to water during prolonged dry spells. The crop will sit happily in the ground until you want to harvest, but the stems are prone to snapping when extracted from frozen soil. If freezing conditions are forecast, lift the leeks beforehand, trim the leaves, wrap them in newspaper and store in a cool place

Parsnips

For the best winter parsnips, sow as soon as the soil has warmed up in spring. They will grow all summer, forming sweet and starchy winter roots.

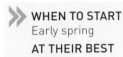

WHEN TO START
Early spring

AT THEIR BEST
Winter

TIME TO COMPLETE
🕐 30 minutes for sowing
3 hours for planting out

YOU WILL NEED
🎯 Parsnip seed
String
Straw
Wire
Plant markers

1 SOW IN DRILLS

Always sow fresh seed. On well-drained soil, mark out a line with string and make a shallow drill, then sow seed thinly along it. Once germinated, thin to 7cm (3in) apart for small, sweet roots, or slightly further apart for larger ones.

2 FROST PROTECTION

In cold weather you may need to apply a straw mulch (pinned down with hoops of wire) to prevent the soil and the parsnips from freezing.

3 HARVEST CROPS

Parsnips taste sweetest after a light frost, so don't harvest too early. The leaves die down in winter, so you will need to mark the rows well so that roots are easily found. Dig up and eat as required; their taste will improve as the winter wears on.

Brussels sprouts

Love them or hate them, no winter vegetable patch is complete without Brussels sprouts. They are big plants that need lots of attention, but they will reward you well.

WHEN TO START
Spring

AT THEIR BEST
Winter

TIME TO COMPLETE
🕐 30 minutes – sowing
3 hours – planting out

YOU WILL NEED
🎯 Brussels sprout seed
Seed trays
Compost
Cage
Fine woven mesh

1 COVER PLANTS

Sow in seed trays and add manure to your beds at the same time. Plant out the seedlings about four weeks later, at least 1m (3ft) apart. Cover plants with a fine mesh to keep out cabbage white butterflies, which lay their eggs on the foliage, as well as pigeons.

2 CROP CARE AND HARVEST

Keep plants well watered until established, and remove withered leaves as they may carry diseases. As they grow, draw up soil around the stems to give them extra stability. Flavour is at its best after a good, hard frost. Harvest sprouts as you need them, picking from the base of the stalk and moving up. After picking all of the sprouts, chop off the top leaves and cook as you would greens.

SELECTIONS >>

Edible flowers

Some flowers can be eaten as well as admired: lavender and roses have a light, perfumed flavour; French marigolds taste spicy; nasturtium peppery; mallow is sweet; and tangy pot marigold petals add a golden hue to food. Most flavours are delicate, and while they may add a subtle taste, edible flowers are most often used as adornments – sweet ones to decorate cakes and puddings, and savoury types sprinkled over salads.

❀❀❀ fully hardy　　❀❀ hardy in mild regions/sheltered sites　　❀ protect from frost over winter
☼ full sun　　☀ partial sun　　✹ full shade　　◊ well-drained soil　　◐ moist soil　　● wet soil

① Wild pansy, *Viola tricolor*; ‡12cm (5in) ↔15cm (6in) ☼ ☀ ◐ ❀❀❀　　**②** Pot marigold, *Calendula officinalis*; ‡50cm (20in) ↔40cm (16in) ☼ ☀ ◊ ❀❀❀　　**③** Bergamot, *Monarda didyma*; ‡90cm (36in) ↔45cm (18in) ☼ ☀ ◐ ❀❀❀　　**④** Rose (scented species), eg *Rosa* 'Summer Wine'; ‡3m (10ft) ↔2.2m (7ft) ☼ ◐ ❀❀❀　**⑤** Lavender, *Lavandula angustifolia*; ‡1m (3ft) ↔1.2m (4ft) ☼ ◊ ❀❀❀　　**⑥** Courgette; ‡45cm (18in) ↔90cm (36in) ☼ ◐ ● ❀❀　　**⑦** Nasturtium, *Tropaeolum majus* Alaska Series; ‡30cm (12in) ↔45cm (18in) ☼ ◐ ❀　　**⑧** *Anchusa azurea* 'Loddon Royalist'; ‡90cm (36in) ↔ 60cm (24in) ☼ ◐ ❀❀❀　　**⑨** Annual mallow, *Malope trifida*; ‡90cm (36in) ↔24cm (10in) ☼ ◐ ❀❀❀
⑩ French marigold, *Tagetes* Gem Series 'Tangerine Gem'; ‡23cm (9in) ↔30cm (12in) ☼ ◊ ❀
Warning: the pollen of some flowers may cause a reaction in those who suffer from asthma or hayfever.

Make a box of herbs and leaves

Growing herbs and salads in a windowbox provides a fresh supply close to the kitchen, and by making a box to your own specifications, you can ensure it fits your space perfectly. All you need are some simple tools and a few basic DIY skills to create this timber design.

 WHEN TO START
Any time

AT ITS BEST
Spring and summer

TIME TO COMPLETE

 4 hours

YOU WILL NEED

Herbs and small lettuce plants
Drill, saw and tape measure
5cm (2in) self-tapping screws
Treated timber
Battens (about 12mm thick)
Copper anti-slug tape
12mm roofing tacks
Multi-purpose compost

1 MEASURE TIMBER
Decide on the length of your windowbox and buy pieces of wood long enough to make two sides, two ends, and a base, and mark them out.

2 CUT INTO LENGTHS
Double-check the measurements and cut out the pieces. To create straight cuts and a neater finish, support both ends of the timber as you saw.

3 SCREW SIDES TOGETHER

Use self-tapping screws to attach one side piece to an end piece; two screws should be enough. If the wood is hard, drill small pilot holes first. Repeat with the other side and end pieces. Screw the two sections together.

4 ATTACH BATTENS TO BASE

Attach the base by screwing it to both side and end pieces. Cut two battens to size, to fit the underside of the box. These will lift the base off the windowsill, allowing space for drainage. Turn the box upside down and attach the battens with short screws.

5 DRILL DRAINAGE HOLES

Good drainage is essential for healthy plants. With the box still upside down, use a drill to make a 1cm (½in) hole every 10cm (4in) along the base of the trough. Take care not to damage the surface below.

6 FIX COPPER TAPE

Attach a band of copper tape around the trough to deter snails, and to provide a decorative finish. Check you have sufficient tape to wrap all the way around without leaving any gaps.

8 PLANT WITH HERBS AND SALAD LEAVES

Fill the trough with compost and plant up with a range of herbs, and a few young lettuce plants. Make sure none of them forms a bridge over the copper tape as they grow, which would enable snails to bypass it and climb in.

7 NAIL TAPE SECURELY

To keep the tape in place, hammer small tacks along it, at 10–15cm (4–6in) intervals. Add more to make a feature of them, if desired. Make sure the tape seam is secure.

Sow a bowl of salad

Salads are "must-grow" vegetables, and taste so much better when picked fresh rather than bought. They are among the easiest of vegetables to grow, require little space, and mature in a few weeks.

Sowing in pots

Grow salad leaves in containers, and you can just step outside and cut them when you need them. Cut-and-come-again leaf crops make the most of limited space and give a ready supply.

>> **WHEN TO START**
Spring and throughout summer
AT ITS BEST
Summer into autumn

TIME TO COMPLETE
 30 minutes

YOU WILL NEED
 Mixed salad leaf seed
Containers
Multi-purpose compost
Scissors

∧ > *Cut and come again*
While it is possible to grow traditional "headed" lettuce in containers, you will get more salad from the space, and a more attractive effect, if you choose leaves that grow back after cutting.

1 CHOOSE A VARIETY
For an attractive and colourful display, and an interesting bowl of salad, look for seed mixes containing a variety of different colours and textures. Lettuce mixes are a good choice early in the season, as they germinate well and grow abundantly in cooler conditions. The cooler night-time temperatures in spring, and lengthening days, can make baby Oriental leaf mixtures flower and go to seed all too quickly; sow these after midsummer. Ensure your containers have drainage holes in the bottom, and cover them with broken clay pieces. Then fill with compost and firm it down.

2 SOW ON SOIL SURFACE
Sow thinly across the surface, cover lightly with compost, and water well. Cut-and-come-again crops can be sown thickly, but you should thin the seedlings to a spacing of about 5cm (2in), once they are large enough to handle.

3 HARVEST THE LEAVES
When the leaves reach about 15cm (6in) high, cut them with a pair of scissors. Keep them fresh until needed in a sealed, moistened, plastic bag. The plants will re-grow several times before they are exhausted and need replacing.

Growing in beds

Beds provide more space than pots, so use them for larger, traditional, headed lettuces, although cut-and-come-again crops will flourish here too.

1 SOW IN DRILLS
Both types of lettuce should be sown in shallow drills. The only difference is that headed lettuce should be sown much more thinly. Once seeds have germinated, thin them out to 15–30cm (6–12in) apart, depending on their final size.

2 TAKE CARE
Protect your plants from slugs using mini cloches made from clear plastic bottles. You may also need to net them to prevent birds eating your crops. Water them regularly during summer. They are prone to bolting in hot weather, so plant them close to taller crops, such as beans, that will provide shade.

Leafy options

Rocket has a strong, piquant taste that gives a kick to milder lettuce-based salads. Lamb's lettuce (corn salad) is a winter crop with a nuttier flavour.

PLANTING AND AFTERCARE
Rocket is best sown in spring and early autumn, when the cooler temperatures make it less likely to bolt. Sow thinly and protect the plants from flea beetles, which nibble the leaves, by covering them with a fine mesh or garden fleece.

Lamb's lettuce can be sown at any time in spring and summer. It is a useful crop to sow late in the season to provide a tasty winter substitute for lettuce. For the best quality leaves, grow lamb's lettuce under cloches, or in a glasshouse or polytunnel.

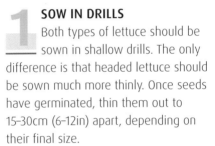

∧ **Tasty leaves**
Lamb's lettuce (top) and rocket will make a tasty addition to your lunchtime sandwiches.

Spring onions

Spring onions fit in almost anywhere, and will germinate quickly and mature between other crops. These shallow-rooted plants will even grow and produce a crop in a seed tray or container.

GROWING AND HARVESTING
Spring onions are an ideal crop for pots and containers. Sprinkle a small amount of seed on the surface of the compost once every two weeks throughout spring and summer, to ensure a constant supply. Spring onions sown in late summer can be left in the soil during winter, to harvest the following spring.

∨ *Pack a punch*
Simply lift the tangy bulbs from the soil as you need them and use in salads or stir-fries.

Salad leaves

With such a wide variety of salads on offer, you can grow leaves for your salad bowl all year round, if you can provide some frost protection in winter. From mild, buttery lettuce to spicy mizuna, oriental mustard and salad rocket, and bitter chicory and endive, salads will never be boring again. You can even snip in a few chives for a hint of onion. Grow a range with different tastes and colours, and provide shelter from hot sun for the best leaves.

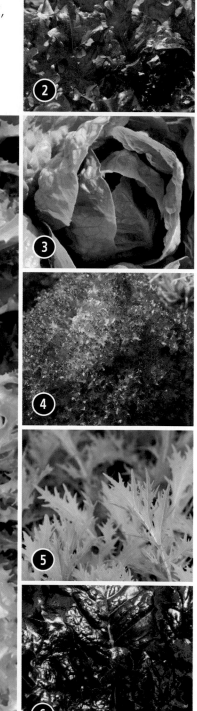

SELECTIONS >>

❀❀❀ fully hardy   ❀❀ hardy in mild regions/sheltered sites   ❀ protect from frost over winter
☼ full sun   ☀ partial sun   ☀ full shade   ◊ well-drained soil   💧 moist soil   💧 wet soil

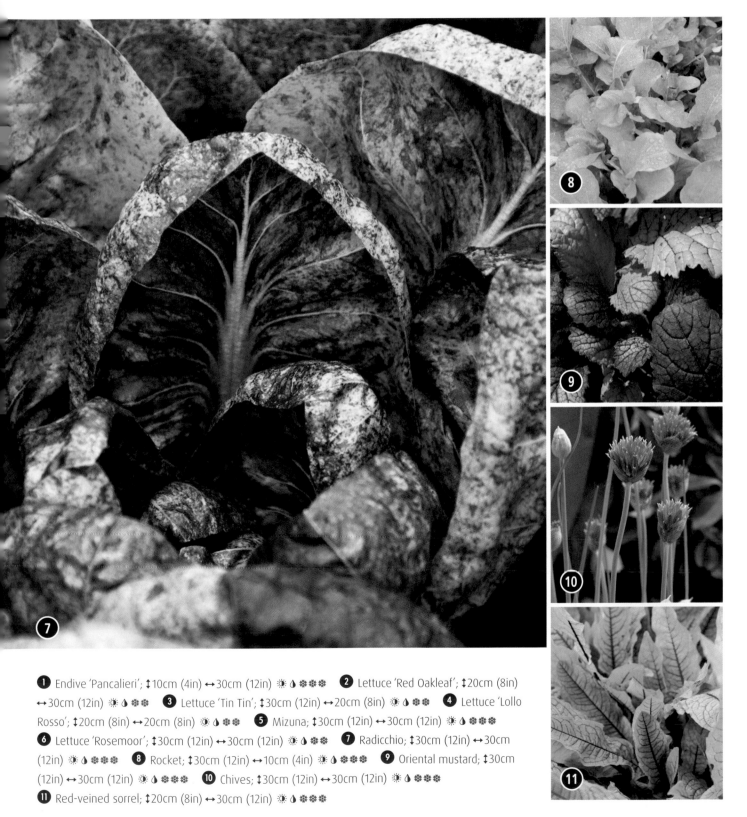

SELECTIONS

❶ Endive 'Pancalieri'; ‡10cm (4in) ↔30cm (12in) ☀💧❀❀❀   ❷ Lettuce 'Red Oakleaf'; ‡20cm (8in) ↔30cm (12in) ☀💧❀❀   ❸ Lettuce 'Tin Tin'; ‡30cm (12in) ↔20cm (8in) ☀💧❀❀   ❹ Lettuce 'Lollo Rosso'; ‡20cm (8in) ↔20cm (8in) ☀💧❀❀   ❺ Mizuna; ‡30cm (12in) ↔30cm (12in) ☀💧❀❀❀   ❻ Lettuce 'Rosemoor'; ‡30cm (12in) ↔30cm (12in) ☀💧❀❀   ❼ Radicchio; ‡30cm (12in) ↔30cm (12in) ☀💧❀❀❀   ❽ Rocket; ‡30cm (12in) ↔10cm (4in) ☀💧❀❀❀   ❾ Oriental mustard; ‡30cm (12in) ↔30cm (12in) ☀💧❀❀❀   ❿ Chives; ‡30cm (12in) ↔30cm (12in) ☀💧❀❀❀   ⓫ Red-veined sorrel; ‡20cm (8in) ↔30cm (12in) ☀💧❀❀❀

Feeding your plants

No matter how good your soil, it will probably need extra nutrients to help plants with specific needs, or to boost them at key times, like flowering. Always follow the instructions on the label, as too much, or the wrong type of fertilizer, can cause problems, such as plants with all leaves and no flowers.

UNDERSTANDING NUTRIENTS

The three basic elements that plants require are nitrogen (N), phosphorus (P) and potassium (K). Nitrogen is needed for leaf and shoot growth, phosphorus for roots, and potassium helps flowers and fruits to develop. Fertilizer manufacturers list the nutrient content as a ratio: a general purpose fertilizer has an N:P:K ratio of 7:7:7, while a tomato feed has a high concentration of potassium to boost fruit production, and a fertilizer for lawns or leafy crops contains mostly nitrogen. Many fertilizers also include various trace elements or micro-nutrients. A plant's nutrient requirements can depend on their phase of growth, with most needing a general boost in the spring, and more potassium as they fruit or flower.

❶ Nitrogen (nitrate) is needed for healthy leaves. ❷ Potassium (potash) boosts the production of flowers and fruit. ❸ For strong root development, choose a fertilizer rich in phosphorus (phosphate).

FERTILIZER CHOICES

Your local garden centre will offer both organic (derived from plants and animals) and inorganic (chemically manufactured) fertilizers. Most are concentrated for convenience and available as liquids, powders that you dilute in water, or granules. Typical examples of organic fertilizers are pelleted chicken manure; blood, fish and bonemeal; liquid seaweed fertilizer; and homemade plant feeds, such as the diluted liquor from a wormery, or fertilizers made from soaking comfrey leaves. Inorganic feeds include sulphate of potash, Growmore and granular rose feeds.

❶ Blood, fish, and bonemeal is a balanced organic fertilizer, applied through the growing season around flowers and vegetables; cease applications in early autumn. ❷ Slow-release granules, activated by warmth and moisture, give a steady supply of nutrients in containers and borders. ❸ Well-rotted manure or garden compost is rich in trace elements and soil-conditioning substances. Dig it in or apply as a surface mulch. ❹ Growmore is a balanced chemical feed used to enrich the soil for sowing or planting, and as a top dressing.

Mulching

Materials spread on top of the ground, usually around plants, are called mulches. They can be practical — feeding the soil, suppressing weeds, retaining moisture, or insulating roots in winter — or mainly decorative, applied for visual effect.

APPLYING ORGANIC MULCHES

Mulches are applied at different times depending on their purpose. For example, bark chips are spread over the soil after planting to suppress weeds. An organic mulch, such as manure, garden compost, chipped bark, or cocoa shells, must be laid over moist soil, either in spring, following autumn and winter rains, or after watering.

Some mulches, especially bark, use up nutrients temporarily as they decompose, so before laying them, apply a nitrogen-rich fertilizer, such as fish meal. Lay organic mulches in a layer 10cm (4in) deep so they continue to provide cover as they slowly decompose and feed the soil. Replenish these mulches every year.

∧ *Moist mulch*
Organic mulches help to retain moisture but if laid too close to plant stems can cause them to rot, so keep them at a safe distance.

∧ *Useful coverings*
Spread landscape fabric over the soil prior to planting to prevent weed growth (left). *Use straw to keep strawberries clean and dry* (right).

PRACTICAL SOLUTIONS

Man-made mulches offer many benefits. Weed membrane or landscape fabric is a semi-permeable material that blocks light but allows moisture through. Use it on low-maintenance beds, or on weed-ridden soil. Lay it before planting and cover with bark, gravel, or a decorative mulch. Black polythene does not allow moisture through, but it warms the soil and kills off weeds when laid over vegetable beds in spring.Straw insulates the soil, and protects tender plants in winter. It is also used to raise crops, such as strawberries, off the ground, reducing fungal and slug problems. A thick layer of straw will protect the roots of vulnerable plants from frost.

DECORATIVE OPTIONS

Mulches that don't decompose are useful as decorative garden surfaces. They are particularly effective when laid over landscape fabric or membrane, which reduces weed growth and helps to prevent soil mixing in with the mulch and spoiling the effect. For a modern feel, try coloured crushed glass or slate shards. Cover small areas, like the tops of pots and containers, with beads, crushed and whole shells, or polished pebbles. Natural cobbles and pebbles blend well with gravel or shingle over larger areas, and can create a beach effect when laid in swathes.

❶ Pebbles and cobbles come in different colours and sizes. Ask to see a sample out of the bag, wetted to show the true colour.
❷ Crushed glass is usually a recycled product, milled to take off the sharp edges. Use bright colours for design highlights.
❸ Slate chips in various grades and subtle shades of dark grey have sharp edges, so are unsuitable for children's areas.
❹ Crushed shells are recycled from the seafood industry.

Watering your plants

All plants need watering, but some need more than others. Concentrate on plants in containers, where the compost dries out relatively quickly; newly planted specimens that haven't yet developed a strong enough root system to cope on their own; and fruits and vegetables at key stages in their growth cycle.

PRESERVE WATER SUPPLIES

Water is a precious commodity, but if you irrigate only those plants that need it, and water in the cool of the morning or in the evening, you can greatly reduce your impact on supplies.

Other ways to minimize water usage are to add moisture-retentive gel crystals to containers, and mulch borders every year after it has rained. Trees, shrubs, and perennials will also need watering less frequently during the first few months if you plant them when the soil is naturally moist in autumn, winter, and early spring. Lay turf in late winter and early spring, too, and it will usually establish well without the need for extra irrigation.

After planting, encourage deep rooting by watering thoroughly and then leaving for 5–7 days before watering again, rather than giving frequent small doses. The water will then sink deep into the soil and encourage roots to follow. Also, if planting in the rain shadow of walls and hedges use drought-tolerant species.

∧ *No buts about water butts*
Save water by installing water butts around your property, connecting them to the rainwater downpipes. Metal or plastic butts are widely available, or choose something more attractive like this wooden barrel.

Watering methods

Make the most of your water supplies and save yourself time and energy by using a watering method that suits the job at hand. A watering can is ideal for small areas where you want to target water accurately; hoses are best for large beds, but use them with care to avoid wastage.

WATERING BY HAND

If you only have a few plants or pots to water, use a watering can, and pour slowly so it has a chance to soak into the roots; remove fine roses from cans unless watering new plantings. Direct water to the roots of your plants — they do not absorb water through their leaves so spraying overhead is not only wasteful but means that less moisture reaches the soil. Also avoid flowers and fruits, which may rot if too wet. Mound up the soil around the base of large plants to create a reservoir in which water will collect and sink down to the root area.

When hosing beds and borders, focus the spray on the soil, and turn it off as you move between planted areas. Long-handled hoses are useful if you have lots of pots and baskets to reach — again, turn the flow off between each container.

∧ *Spraying from a distance*
Long-handled hoses allow you to reach hanging baskets with ease, and also to direct water to less accessible plants, such as vegetables in a large bed, without treading on the soil.

AUTOMATIC SYSTEMS

Relatively easy to install, automatic watering systems can save hours of work in the garden; attach a timer, and they will water your plot in your absence. Most come in kit form and allow you to design a system that suits your garden. Kits typically include a network of main pipes into which you insert fine feeder pipes that take water directly to individual plants or pots. These terminate in small drip nozzles, held just above soil level, that gradually release water, which drains down around the roots. Check your watering system every few weeks to ensure plants aren't being under- or over-watered, and adjust individual flow regulators as necessary. Turn off nozzles when no longer required.

< Timed to perfection
Set water timers to come on every day or week, in the morning or evening to minimize evaporation, and alter the program if the weather changes.

LEAKY AND SEEP HOSES

Less sophisticated than automatic irrigation systems, these perforated hosepipes are perfect for watering lots of plants at the same time. Unlike a regular hosepipe, water gradually seeps out at soil level and penetrates deeply. Lay one along a row of thirsty vegetables, or weave it between newly planted shrubs and perennials. Attach the hose to a water butt, which may need to be raised up to provide a gravitational flow of water, or fit on to an outdoor tap. Lift your hose and reposition it as needed.

Slow-release watering >
The most efficient watering method if used correctly, seep hoses trickle water into the soil exactly where it is needed.

WATERING CONTAINERS

Although large containers need watering less frequently than small ones, they may still require water every day in summer. Porous terracotta pots dry out quickly, so consider lining them with plastic before planting. Don't rely on rain to water your pots as the compost often remains dry after a shower. When planting, leave a gap of at least 2cm (1in) between the compost and the pot's rim to allow water to collect there. A bark or gravel mulch helps retain moisture.

< Preventing soil erosion
Direct water onto a piece of broken pot to help prevent compost being washed off the roots.

TOP TIP: WATERING TREES

Help trees to establish by inserting perforated drainage tubing into the hole, close to the roots, at planting time. Water poured into the exposed end is directed to the root area with no wastage. Mulch, or use a tree mat, to deter weeds and to seal in moisture.

Create a beautiful bog garden

Some of the most fabulous plants will only grow in soil that is permanently moist, and even if you don't have a boggy area in your garden, it is quite easy to create one. This type of planting looks particularly natural next to ponds or among trees, but can be equally effective in any part of the garden.

WHEN TO START
Anytime
AT ITS BEST
Summer

TIME TO COMPLETE
 2 days

YOU WILL NEED
 Hosepipe
Pond liner
Bricks
Gravel
Well-rotted organic matter, such
 as farmyard manure
Topsoil
Perforated hose
Scissors
Rake
Fork
Spade
Bog plants

1 DIG OUT BORDER
Next to your pond or other suitable area, use a garden hose to make a curved and natural outline for your bog garden. Dig it out to a depth of about 60cm (24in) and keep the soil.

2 PLACE LINER AND STABILIZE

Lay the liner in the hole and push it into the corners. To hold it in place, overlap the edges of the hole with at least 30cm (12in) of liner, and weigh it down with bricks. Make sure the liner is not pulled tight or it could rip when filled.

3 PERFORATE LINER WITH FORK

Although you want the soil in your bog garden to be moist, it should not be completely saturated or it will lack oxygen, which is vital for healthy plant roots. To provide some drainage, pierce the liner with a garden fork at 1m (3ft) intervals.

4 COVER BASE WITH GRAVEL

To ensure that the drainage holes do not become blocked over time, causing the soil in your bog garden to stagnate, cover the liner with a layer of gravel or coarse grit. A depth of about 8cm (3in) thick should be sufficient.

5 TRIM EDGE OF LINER

Fill the bog garden with the soil you excavated when digging the hole, together with some well-rotted organic matter, and press it down. This will settle the liner into its final position. Use sharp scissors to cut any visible excess liner from around the edges.

6 PLACE PERFORATED HOSE ROUND PERIMETER

A perforated hose, which allows water to seep out slowly, will make it easier to keep your bog garden topped up during dry periods. Sink it into the soil all the way around the inside edge of the bog garden, just leaving the hose attachment above ground. You can then simply attach a garden hose to it when necessary. As the hose attachment will eventually be hidden by plants, remember to mark its position in the garden.

7 PLANT UP

Lay your bog plants out in their pots, and when you are happy with the design, plant them so that they are at the same level as in their pots, or slightly deeper. Mulch with organic matter. Keep well watered until the plants are fully established.

Striking bog plants

The plants that thrive in boggy conditions are as varied and colourful as any other group, and there are many attractive effects you can create by choosing carefully. Several have impressive and boldly-shaped foliage for maximum drama, including giant rhubarb-like *Gunnera*, hand-shaped *Rodgersia* and golden-leaved *Carex*. Others, such as *Iris sibirica* and *Primula japonica,* bring a more refined and delicate beauty to your bog garden.

✳✳✳ fully hardy ✳✳ hardy in mild regions/sheltered sites ✳ protect from frost over winter
☀ full sun ☀ partial sun ☀ full shade ◌ well-drained soil ◖ moist soil ● wet soil

❶ Arum lily, *Zantedeschia aethiopica*; ↕90cm (36in) ↔90cm (36in) ☀ ◖ ✳ ❷ *Darmera peltata*;
↕1.9m (6ft) ↔1m (3ft) ☀ ☀ ◖ ✳✳✳ ❸ *Carex elata* 'Aurea'; ↕70cm (28in) ↔ 45cm (18in) ☀ ☀ ◖ ✳✳✳
❹ *Iris sibirica* 'Shirley Pope'; ↕80cm (32in) ↔45cm (18in) ☀ ☀ ◖ ✳✳✳ ❺ *Rodgersia sambucifolia*;
↕90cm (36in) ↔90cm (36in) ☀ ☀ ● ✳✳✳ ❻ *Primula japonica* 'Miller's Crimson'; ↕45cm (18in)
↔45cm (18in) ☀ ☀ ◖ ✳✳✳ ❼ Globeflower, *Trollius europaeus*; ↕80cm (32in) ↔45cm (18in)
☀ ☀ ◖ ✳✳✳ ❽ *Filipendula purpurea*; ↕1.2m (4ft) ↔ 60cm (24in) ☀ ☀ ◖ ✳✳✳ ❾ *Gunnera
manicata*; ↕2.5m (8ft) ↔3m (10ft) ☀ ☀ ◖ ✳✳✳ ❿ *Eupatorium purpureum*; ↕2m (6ft) ↔1m (3ft)
☀ ☀ ◖ ✳✳✳ ⓫ *Ligularia stenocephala* 'The Rocket'; ↕1.5m (5ft) ↔1m (3ft) ☀ ☀ ◖ ✳✳✳

Trim a simple topiary

Topiary lends structure and formality to any planting scheme, and makes a useful focal point, whether grown in a container or planted directly into the border. All you need to bring an overgrown specimen back into shape, or to make a cone from scratch, are some basic tools, patience, and a good eye.

>> **WHEN TO START**
Summer

AT ITS BEST
All year round

TIME TO COMPLETE
 1 hour

YOU WILL NEED
 One box plant, *Buxus sempervirens*
Household disinfectant
Sharp long-handled shears

1 SELECT A HEALTHY PLANT
When choosing a specimen to clip into topiary, look for one with dense, healthy growth, unblemished foliage, and a strong leading stem in the centre.

2 START TO TRIM BY EYE
Looking down on the plant, locate the central stem, which will form the top of the cone. With shears, trim around the stem to create the outline.

3 KEEP MOVING AROUND THE PLANT
Don't trim the topiary in "sides", as you risk over-clipping one area. Continually move around the plant, regularly taking a step back to look at the overall shape.

4 ASSESS SHAPE FROM TOP
When you have nearly finished, look down at the central stem to check that the outline of the cone is straight and even. Assess the shape all the way around, and trim accordingly.

5 ROUTINE CARE
Established topiary should be pruned once or twice a year in midsummer and early autumn. Never clip on hot, sunny days to prevent the newly exposed foliage from being scorched.

Tool choices

Creating topiary shapes is much easier if you have the right tools, and always keep the blades sharp and clean. Although you can use garden shears to trim cones and simple shapes, long-handled shears (*far left*) are a better choice as they offer greater control. For more intricate designs, use topiary shears (*below*).

TOP TIP: CLEAN CUTS

Box blight is a major disease affecting box (*Buxus sempervirens*), which is commonly used for topiary. Protect your specimens by cleaning your pruning shears between plants with a spray of household disinfectant.

< *Points of view*
Slim topiary cones provide structure in this small mixed border, as well some vertical emphasis.

Build a decorative edge

Edging is both practical and aesthetic. At its most useful it marks out the boundary of a lawn, while also allowing you to simply run the mower over it. With a wide variety of materials to choose from, edging can be a decorative feature in its own right, chosen to complement the plants it contains.

 WHEN TO START
Any time

AT ITS BEST
All year round

TIME TO COMPLETE

 5 hours

YOU WILL NEED

Bricks
String and pegs
Sharp spade
Wet mortar mix
Dry mortar mix
Rubber mallet
Spirit level
Trowel
Brush

1 USE STRING AS A GUIDE
Use one brick to measure the correct distance from your raised bed (or border) and set up a line of string between two pegs from which to work. Cut through the turf along the line using the sharp edge of a spade.

2 REMOVE A STRIP OF TURF
Dig out a strip of turf deep enough to accommodate the bricks plus a 2.5cm (1in) layer of mortar. First slice the turf up into manageable sections, then slide the spade underneath and lift them out onto a piece of tarpaulin.

3 LEVEL THE GROUND
Use the spade to roughly level out the ground. Mix wet mortar and add a 2.5cm (1in) layer to the bottom of the trench to bed in the bricks.

4 LAY BRICKS ON MORTAR
Place the bricks on the mortar and set slightly below the level of the turf. Leave a small gap between each. Use a spirit level to check they are horizontal, and firm them using a rubber mallet.

5 APPLY A DRY MIX
Finally use a dry mortar mix to fill the joints between the bricks, working the mixture in with a trowel. Clean off the excess with a brush.

Edging options

Different edging materials will bring different looks to your garden, from delicate and ephemeral to solid and hard working. Copper piping, bent into a graceful curve (*above*), provides a pretty edge that echoes the colours of the planting.

❶ In an informal area, allow your plants to spill over onto solid brick paving.
❷ Geometric Victorian-style brick edging suits both formal and cottage-style gardens. ❸ The attractive soft grey of slate chippings provides a perfect foil for edging plants. ❹ Log edging is the ideal choice for seaside-themed gardens, especially when used with a shingle mulch, mixed with larger pebbles.

Make a family garden

Creating a plot that children and parents will both enjoy is not easy. The key is to provide kids with space to play without filling it with garish toys, while setting aside a relaxing area for grown-ups to chill.

∧ *Green fingers*
Children enjoy the responsibility of looking after their own projects, so why not encourage them to grow some fruit and vegetables, and learn how plants develop?

COMBINING PLAY WITH PLANTING

Research shows that children and adults benefit mentally and physically from being in a natural environment. So although it is tempting to buy a plastic play gym and set it in the centre of the lawn, it may not be very beneficial for your children in the long run. Instead, surround play areas with plants that children will enjoy, such as cheerful sunflowers and those that attract butterflies, such as *Buddleja*.

Children's interests change rapidly, and what they like one year will be passed over the next. Prevent boredom setting in by providing toys that are not permanent fixtures, and will seem new and exciting time after time. Tents are a great choice, appealing to all ages, and offering limitless opportunities for imaginative play. All you need is an area of lawn to pitch one on.

Growing fruit and vegetables allows children to take a real interest in gardening; sowing seeds and watching their plants grow gives young ones a real sense of achievement. Plastic sandpits often languish unloved once the novelty has worn off, but one made from a raised bed can be easily converted into a small vegetable plot, the perfect size for little hands to tend their first crops.

∧ *Raise your play*
This sandpit is made from a timber raised bed, which you can buy as a kit, or make yourself (see pp.58–59). When children tire of the sand, fill the bed with colourful sunflowers, edible flowers, such as nasturtiums, and quick-growing vegetables.

TOP TIP: SIMPLE SWINGS

You can make a simple swing from a thick rope attached securely to a sturdy tree branch. Tie an old tyre to it to make a traditional swing, checking that it will hold your child by swinging on it yourself first. Alternatively, knot the rope at intervals for children to climb up. Adult supervision is always advisable when small children are using any type of play equipment.

∧ *Swing seat*
Play equipment need not be expensive or shop-bought. A rope and old tyre are all you need to keep children happy. Just make sure your child is strong enough to hold on to the rope when swinging.

Water and wildlife

If your children can swim and are old enough to understand the dangers of water, ponds offer more play opportunities than almost any other garden feature. They are easy to build and will soon attract a wealth of wildlife to your garden.

BE SAFE

Small children can drown in just a few centimetres of water, so wait until yours are old enough to appreciate the dangers before installing a water feature. If you have older children with younger siblings, fit a custom-made metal grille over the water surface and ensure it will take the weight of a child, should he or she fall.

WILDLIFE HAVEN

As soon as your pond is installed, birds and small animals will visit to drink and bathe, and many other creatures will become permanent residents. Make sure the sides are sloped so they can get out if they fall in, and plant around the sides to provide them with cover and habitats. Frogs and toads will be drawn to any pond, large or small, and in spring will fill the water with spawn. Other creatures to look out for include water beetles, pond skaters, water snails, newts, damselflies and dragonflies.

∧ **Aquatic homes**
Wrap planting around your pond to create shelter for wildlife, such as birds, small mammals, frogs, and toads.

< **Beauty and the beast**
Look out for dragonfly nymphs as they climb from the water and shed their skins, before emerging as adults.

Plots for pets

Sharing your garden with pets can be a fun and fulfilling experience, and by catering for their needs, as well as your own, you can all live happily together in the same plot.

PET SPACES

Small pets, such as guinea pigs and rabbits, are happiest in a secure run on a lawn. If you move the run every few days, you may even eliminate the need to mow the grass altogether.

Dogs who have free reign of the garden can present problems if they are not trained. Set aside a quiet area, such as behind a shed, for your dog to use as a toilet. After a few weeks, and treats for good behaviour, he or she will only go there. Raised beds and borders edged with low hedging will also help deter your dog from rampaging through your favourite flowers.

Cats are not as easily trained as dogs, especially in their toilet habits. Encourage them to use a litter tray, and deter them from using the borders by inserting short pieces of cane in the areas where they are likely to dig. Cats like bare soil, so these are the areas to concentrate on.

< **Dog territory**
Boisterous dogs can devastate gardens by trampling plants, so grow your favourites in raised beds to help reduce the risk. Also, weigh down containers to stop them from being knocked over.

Kitty treat >
Cats adore the scent of catmint (Nepeta) and love to roll around in it. Give your pet a treat and set aside a bed for this pretty plant.

Homes for birds and bees

Birds and beneficial insects not only make a garden a more interesting place, they also help to control pests and improve flower pollination. Gardening organically helps make them feel welcome, but providing a specially made home really rolls out the red carpet and encourages them to stay.

Bee hotel

Solitary bees are excellent pollinators, but they can struggle to find nesting sites. A home-made nest looks attractive and provides them with shelter, as well as ensuring you have bumper harvests.

>> **WHEN TO START**
Summer

AT ITS BEST
Autumn to winter

TIME TO COMPLETE
🕐 30 minutes

YOU WILL NEED
🛈 Secateurs
Bamboo canes
Modelling clay
Raffia or string
Small terracotta or plastic pot

1 CUT LENGTHS OF BAMBOO
Use sharp secateurs to cut short lengths of bamboo cane that will fit into your pot. The natural variation in diameter will attract different bee species.

2 PUSH THEM INTO A POT
Fill the base of a terracotta pot with modelling clay and push the cut bamboo canes firmly into it. Continue doing this until the pot is packed tightly.

3 HANG YOUR HOTEL
Tie raffia or string firmly around the pot and suspend it from a hook or attach it to a wall. Choose a sheltered, sunny site, and angle the open end of the pot downwards so that the bamboo canes do not fill up with water when it rains.

TOP TIP: FLOWER FOOD

To make life even better for your resident bees, position the nest close to a border planted with nectar-rich flowers. They will then have only a short distance to travel for food, which will be a great help to them in spring.

Choosing and siting a nest

Encourage birds to visit your garden and you will have a ready army of pest-eaters on your side. If you can persuade them to make their nests and rear their young there too, they will make a fascinating animated addition to the flowers and foliage. Put up one or two nest boxes, and see who moves in.

CHOOSING THE RIGHT BOX

Birds are picky about where they live, so it is important to choose the right type of box. Select one that is made from an insulating material, such as wood or woodcrete to prevent them from becoming too hot or cold, and avoid any made from ceramic or those with metal roofs. Correct hole size is also important: too small, and the birds you want to attract may not fit; too large, and wind, rain, and even predators may get in. The box should be robust, waterproof, safe, and comfortable. Different bird species have different needs, so if you want to make a home for a particular type of bird, do some research first and find out what suits it.

SITING YOUR BOX

Nest boxes should be sited in a sheltered place, away from strong sunlight, wind and rain. Position them in the quietest area of the garden, away from feeding areas, and at least 1.5m (5ft) above the ground. This mimics the nesting places birds naturally prefer, and keeps them safe from predators. Choose a position away from large branches where cats can lurk, but where there are flimsy twigs nearby to give fledglings somewhere to perch when they first leave the nest. The best time to put up nest boxes is outside the breeding season, between midsummer and late winter.

❶ Birds use roosting pockets to hide from predators during the day. Smaller species, such as wrens, may even nest in them.
❷ Boxes with a smaller 25mm hole, are attractive to a wide range of garden birds, including blue tits, coal tits, and marsh tits.
❸ Open-fronted nest boxes appeal to robins, wrens, and pied wagtails, who prefer to see out of their home.

TOP TIP: HOME-MADE BOX

If you want to make your own bird box, wood is probably the easiest and best material to use. There are plenty of plans and designs available to follow that only require simple tools and basic carpentry skills. Wood needs to be treated to stop it decaying, and you may also decide to stain or paint it. In all cases, choose products that are non-toxic and wildlife-friendly to help keep your birds healthy.

Composting essentials

Composting conveniently disposes of your garden cuttings and trimmings, while at the same time creating a free, and wonderful, soil improver. It can be as simple as throwing all your waste into a pile and forgetting about it, but you will get better results if you follow a few simple guidelines.

CHOOSING A BIN

Bog standard plastic compost bins are functional, rather than attractive, but do hold lots of garden and kitchen waste. They are also the most inexpensive, and can often be bought at a discounted price through your local council. If you are concerned about how your compost bin fits in with the rest of the garden, there are more attractive options, including wooden bins designed to look like bee hives that can be stained to suit your garden design. These are a good choice for smaller gardens where the bin would be on view. Impatient gardeners may prefer "tumbler" bins. These allow you to make small batches of compost in weeks, not months, by turning the bin to increase airflow, which naturally speeds up the composting process.

∧ *Types of compost bin (clockwise from top left)*
A standard plastic compost bin, the sort available from local councils; an attractive, wooden bin, designed to look like a beehive; a vertical "tumbler" type, suitable for smaller amounts of compost; a horizontal "tumbler" bin, designed for easy turning.

FILLING YOUR BIN

To produce good compost it is important to have the right mix of ingredients. If you add too much soft, green material, such as grass clippings, the heap may turn into a slimy, smelly sludge. Put in too much dry, woody material, and it will rot down slowly, if at all. Ideally aim for a ratio of about 50:50. During most of the year, it is likely that you will be producing more green than dry material, so you will need to search around for dry waste to add. Woody prunings are best, but brown cardboard, crumpled newspaper, and even the insides of used toilet rolls all make suitable alternatives.

QUICKENING THE PACE

Air is essential to the composting process, so the contents must be turned regularly to ensure good airflow throughout your bin or heap. Turning also allows you to check how things are going, to wet the mix if it is too dry, or to add dry material if it is too wet. This task is easier if you have two bins, but if you only have one, simply empty it out onto a tarpaulin, mix the contents well, then refill the bin.

TOP TIP: BOKASHI COMPOSTING

Cooked foods, meat, and fish should never be composted in an ordinary bin as they attract rats and harmful bacteria. Instead, compost this type of waste using the Japanese bokashi system. This involves using a special sealed bin that you fill in layers, each one sprinkled with bran dust, inoculated with micro-organisms. The content of the bin then effectively pickles, and after about two weeks, it can be emptied out and buried in the garden or added to the compost heap. This method also produces a liquor that can be diluted and used as a liquid feed.

The bokashi bin >
Food scraps pickle in the sealed bin for two weeks and give off very little smell. The bin can be kept indoors or outside.

Make a bin

A home-made bin is just as good as a bought one, and you can make it whatever size and shape that best suits your garden, and the quantity of material you want to compost.

TIME TO COMPLETE

🕐 1 day

YOU WILL NEED

🔧 4 posts about 1.5m (5ft) long
Mallet
Chicken wire
Fencing staples
Cardboard boxes
Old carpet

1 ATTACH WIRE TO POSTS

Set the posts 75cm (30in) apart in a square and drive them 30cm (12in) into the ground, using a mallet. Wrap the chicken wire around the posts and attach it with fencing staples. Snip off excess wire, and make sure that no sharp strands are left sticking out.

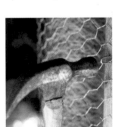

2 ADD CARDBOARD SIDES

Flatten the cardboard boxes and put several layers on each side, slotting them between the posts and the netting. Put a layer on the base then start filling your bin. Place a piece of old carpet on top of the waste; replace it each time you add more. This helps keep out the rain and insulates the bin, speeding up the composting process.

Plant a shady border

A border set in deep shade can be a real bonus in the garden if you choose your plants carefully, as some of the most beautiful shrubs will only grow well in low light conditions. These areas may lack the drama of a sunny spot, but they have a cool and understated sophistication of their own.

 WHEN TO START
Autumn

AT ITS BEST
Spring

TIME TO COMPLETE

 2 hours for preparation
3 hours for planting

YOU WILL NEED

 Spade
Organic matter, such as
  well-rotted leafmould

Shrubs such as:
Camellia and flowering currant,
  Ribes sanguineum.
Underplanting, for example
  Bergenia, Dicentra spectabilis,
ferns and hellebores.

1 BEFORE YOU PLANT
Many plants that enjoy living in shady conditions grow naturally in woodlands, and need a cool, moist soil, which has been enriched with leafmould. In autumn, clear the area of all weeds, then mix plenty of leafmould into the soil (*to make leafmould, see pp.126–127*).

2 DIG PLANTING HOLES
Buy your shrubs in autumn or spring, and plan carefully where you are going to plant them, taking into account their final size. The shrubs go towards the back of the border, with the underplanting below them, and in front. The planting holes should be twice as wide and slightly deeper than the pots.

3 CHECK PLANTING DEPTHS
Put some leafmould in the bottom of each hole and then place a plant on top of it. Use a cane across the hole to check the plant will be at the same depth as it was in its original pot when planted.

4 WATER IN WELL
Fill in around the plant with soil and leafmould, and water in well. Water regularly until the plant is established. Mulch with organic matter, like leafmould, leaving the area around the stems clear.

TOP TIP: FEEDING SHRUBS

Shrubs need regular feeding to thrive. Early spring is the best time to sprinkle a fertilizer, such as blood, fish and bone meal, around the base of the plants. Repeat each year to keep growth vigorous and healthy.

Planting options

Shade-tolerant shrubs that are grown for their flowers, such as camellias, need a little light. The selection below is best planted where some sun can filter through, such as near deciduous trees or a trellis.

❶ *Daphne laureola* subsp. *philippi*; ↕45cm (18in) ↔60cm (24in)   ❷ *Rosa rugosa* 'Rubra'; ↕↔2m (6ft)   ❸ *Paeonia delavayi* var. *lutea*; ↕2m (6ft) ↔1.2m (4ft)   ❹ *Hydrangea aspera* Villosa Group; ↕↔3m (10ft)

< Kept in the dark
This beautiful white form of flowering currant, Ribes sanguineum, *and pink camellia are underplanted with a golden-leaved bleeding heart,* Dicentra spectabilis *'Gold Heart', and other shade-lovers.*

Make a shady rockery

Transform a dull, shady corner into a rockery for spring interest. Many shade-loving plants, such as ferns, ivies, and violas, love the cool, moist but well-drained conditions and will thrive here.

≫ **WHEN TO START**
Autumn

AT ITS BEST
Spring

TIME TO COMPLETE
 6 hours: preparation and planting

YOU WILL NEED
 Topsoil (if not working on a sloping site)
Attractive large stones
Bugle, *Ajuga reptans*
Creeping phlox, *Phlox stolonifera*
Dog's-tooth violet, *Erythronium*
Hardy ferns
Hostas
Ivies, *Hedera*
Violas

1 PREPARE THE SOIL
If you have a flat site, create a slope with weed-free topsoil in autumn, so it has time to settle. If you have a slope already, weed it thoroughly. Dig in some grit if the drainage is poor.

2 SELECT AND PLACE STONES
Set rocks into the soil, with larger ones at the base of the slope and smaller ones at the top. Bury one third of each stone, and angle them so that rain will run off into the soil.

3 CHECK PLANTING POSITIONS
In spring, buy your shade-loving plants. Arrange them around the rockery, while they are still in their pots, to see where they will look best, before deciding on their final planting positions.

4 PLANT AND MULCH
Plant in the pockets between the stones, then water well. Mulch with composted bark, or similar, to help keep moisture sealed in and to suppress weeds. Water regularly for the first year.

Versatile ferns

Ferns are a wonderful choice for shady areas. They will grow in the tiniest of dank crevices, as long as they have enough moisture and a glimmer of light. Sunken pits echo the way ferns sometimes lodge themselves in subterranean drains, and peer up from the gloom. You can also try growing them under a bench, where little else will thrive. For dry sites under trees or close to walls, try the male fern, *Dryopteris filix-mas*, or the evergreen hart's tongue fern, *Asplenium scolopendrium*. The royal fern, *Osmunda regalis*, is perfect for damp areas and looks very effective planted near water.

∧ *Cool perspective*
Ferns don't mind shade, so grow them where little else will thrive, such as under garden furniture.

< *Star performers*
Ferns are ideal for these mesh-covered troughs, which were designed as a green car-parking bay.

Dry shade solutions

Shady, dry areas, such as those beneath trees and large shrubs, are some of the trickiest for plants to cope with. Choose sun-lovers for these sites and you will have mean, dried-out plants stretching for light. However, there are a few stalwarts that will not only cope, but thrive in such a spot. To give them a head start, dig large planting holes and mix plenty of well-rotted manure with the soil, then apply lots of water while they settle in.

✿✿✿ fully hardy   ✿✿ hardy in mild regions/sheltered sites   ✿ protect from frost over winter

☀ full sun   ☀ partial sun   ☀ full shade   ◌ well-drained soil   ◐ moist soil   ◆ wet soil

❶ *Kerria japonica* 'Golden Guinea'; ‡2m (6ft) ↔2.4m (8ft) ☀ ☀ ◌ ✿✿✿   ❷ Deadnettle, *Lamium maculatum* 'White Nancy'; ‡15cm (6in) ↔1m (3ft) ☀ ☀ ◌ ◆ ✿✿✿   ❸ Lungwort, *Pulmonaria* 'Lewis Palmer'; ‡35cm (14in) ↔ 45cm (18in) ☀ ☀ ◐ ✿✿✿   ❹ *Saxifraga stolonifera* 'Tricolor'; ‡30cm (12in) ↔30cm (12in) ☀ ☀ ◌ ◐ ✿✿   ❺ *Brunnera macrophylla* 'Dawson's White'; ‡45cm (18in) ↔ 60cm (24in) ☀ ☀ ◌ ◐ ✿✿✿   ❻ *Viburnum davidii*; ‡1.5m (5ft) ↔1.5m (5ft) ☀ ☀ ◌ ◐ ✿✿✿   ❼ *Cyclamen coum* Pewter Group; ‡8cm (3in) ↔10cm (4in) ☀ ☀ ◌ ✿✿✿   ❽ Jacob's ladder, *Polemonium caeruleum*; ‡60cm (24in) ↔30cm (12in) ☀ ☀ ◌ ◐ ✿✿✿   ❾ *Euonymus fortunei* 'Emerald 'n' Gold'; ‡60cm (24in) ↔90cm (36in) ☀ ◐ ✿✿✿   ❿ *Aquilegia vulgaris* 'Nivea'; ‡90cm (36in) ↔ 45cm (18in) ☀ ☀ ◌ ◐ ✿✿✿   ⓫ Fringe cups, *Tellima grandiflora*; ‡80cm (32in) ↔30cm (12in) ☀ ☀ ◌ ◐ ✿✿✿

Grow year-round salads

Growing cress and sprouting seeds indoors provides a constant supply of fresh ingredients for salads and sandwiches all year round. Sow cress every couple of weeks, and prepare jars of sprouts on a daily basis. These easy projects are ideal for children, who love to watch the plants develop.

2 WATER THE POTS

Repeat for several pots – you will need a few if growing for salads. Set the pots on a plant tray or saucers, and water them to dampen the towels.

Easy cress

One packet of seed will be sufficient for a few sowings. Reseal the packet after use and store in a container in the fridge.

TIME TO COMPLETE

30 minutes

YOU WILL NEED

Cress seed
Small pots
Kitchen paper towels
Non-toxic felt-tip pen
All-purpose compost
Plastic bags

1 FOLD KITCHEN TOWEL

Fold a sheet of kitchen towel in four. Invert a pot over it and draw around the rim with a pen. Cut out the circles of paper. Fill the pot with compost to just below the rim and place the four paper circles on top.

3 SOW THE SEEDS

Sprinkle some seeds onto the paper. Place each pot in a plastic bag, seal loosely and store in a cool dark place. When the seedlings are 1cm (½in), remove the bag. Set pots on a windowsill out of direct sun, and keep moist until the cress is ready.

Crunchy sprouts

Delicious and packed with nutrients, sprouting beans add crunchy texture to salads, and you can choose from many different varieties. From spicy onion to mild broccoli, you will find a taste to suit, or try a few and mix them together.

TIME TO COMPLETE

 5 minutes each day

YOU WILL NEED

Packets of beans or seeds
Sprouting jars with lids or tiered sprouters
Storage containers

VARIETIES TO TRY

Adzuki
Alfalfa
Beet
Broccoli
Chickpea
Fenugreek
Lentil
Mung
Onion
Red cabbage
Rocket
Snow peas
Wheatgrass

1 CLEAN THE CONTAINER

Proprietary sprouting jars with meshed lids and tiered sprouters are widely available from garden centres and DIY stores. Make sure you clean them thoroughly before each use. Then pour seeds into your jar (or sprouter), fill it with water, and leave the seeds to soak for 8–10 hours.

2 RINSE AND DRAIN

After soaking, invert the jar over the sink and allow the water to drain out. Rinse the seeds again in fresh cold water and drain again. Make sure there is no water left in the bottom of the jar, and place it in a light area out of direct sun.

3 KEEP RINSING

Rinse and drain the seeds with cold water twice a day to keep them clean and moist. Many seeds sprout and are ready to eat in four or five days. When they are ready, give the sprouts a final rinse, drain, and leave for eight hours to allow excess water to evaporate.

4 STORE AND USE

When the sprouts are dry, use them immediately, or you can store them in the fridge for up to five days. If any go mouldy, discard the whole batch. You can also store the beans in a dark cupboard which will produce white sprouts that have a slightly different flavour to the green ones grown in light.

Plant a bed of spring bulbs

Harbingers of spring, bulbs transform sleeping gardens into oceans of colour as the seasons turn. Starting with the first brave snowdrops that peek through the soil in winter, and closing with a spectacular display of tulips and alliums at the end of spring, bulbs provide a long period of interest. Plant them in autumn – leave tulips until late in the season – and they will flower the following year.

WHEN TO START
Mid-autumn

AT ITS BEST
Early to late spring

TIME TO COMPLETE

🕐 30 minutes for planting

YOU WILL NEED

Fork
Spade
Horticultural grit
Bulb planter or trowel
Chicken wire
Selection of spring bulbs

1 PREPARE TO PLANT

All bulbs need well-drained soil, so if you have heavy clay, either dig in plenty of grit before you start, or grow them in pots. You can either plant bulbs individually, using a bulb planter or trowel, or dig a wide hole and plant them *en masse*, which is an easier method, and more naturalistic.

2 DIG A HOLE

Dig to a depth of about two to four times the height of your bulbs (*see right*). Place the bulbs in the planting hole with the pointed growing tip facing upwards. Discard any bulbs that are mouldy or soft.

3 COVER BULBS

Fill in the hole with soil, taking care not to damage the growing tips, and firm it down with your fingers. Cover with chicken wire to prevent animals digging up the bulbs; remove it when the first shoots appear.

TOP TIP: PLANTING SNOWDROPS

Snowdrops have tiny bulbs that dehydrate quickly, and often fail to flower if planted in autumn. Instead, buy pot-grown bulbs in leaf in the spring and plant them so that the pale bases of the stems are just below the soil surface. If you already have large clumps of snowdrops, lift and divide them in spring, after flowering.

How deep?

For bulbs to succeed, you need to plant them at the right depth, usually two to four times the height of the bulb. Plant too shallowly, and they may not flower; too deep and they might not grow at all.

❶ Tulips prefer to be planted deeply, four times their own depth; 5cm (2in) bulbs are planted 20cm (8in) deep. ❷ Daffodils are planted three times their own depth; 5cm (2in) bulbs are planted 15cm (6in) deep.
❸ Plant grape hyacinths (*Muscari*) at three times their depth; 2cm (¾in) bulbs are planted at a depth of 6cm (2½in).
❹ Alliums are also planted at three times their depth; 3cm (1¼in) bulbs should be planted 9cm (3½in) deep.

Plant a modern rose garden

Create a contemporary display using disease-resistant roses, such as 'Winchester Cathedral' (*below*), and pretty perennials for a modern mix of flowers and foliage. This classic white scheme is easy to plant and maintain; just follow the steps here for the rose, and on pages 47 for the other plants.

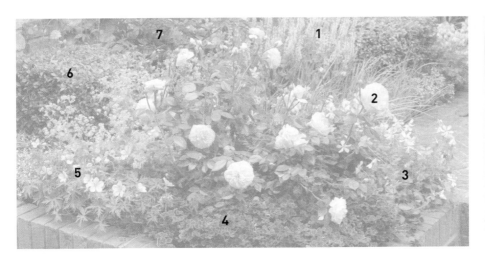

>> **WHEN TO PLANT**
Autumn or early spring
AT ITS BEST
Early to midsummer

TIME TO COMPLETE
🕐 3 hours

YOU WILL NEED
Spade
Heavy-duty gloves
Bamboo cane
Well-rotted organic matter

All-purpose granular fertilizer
Mycorrhizal fungi, eg, Rootgrow

1. *Veronica spicata* 'Alba'
2. *Rosa* Winchester Cathedral ('Auscat')
3. White violas
4. *Trifolium repens* 'Purpurascens Quadrifolium'
5. Hardy white geranium
6. *Alchemilla mollis*
7. *Actaea simplex* 'Brunette'

PREPARE TO PLANT
Dig a bucketful of organic matter into your proposed planting area, and mix it evenly with the soil. Then dig a hole a little deeper and twice as wide as the pot that contains the rose.

CHECK PLANTING DEPTH
Place the rose in its container into the hole, and using a bamboo cane, check that the graft union (the swelling at the base of the stems) will be below the soil surface when the rose is planted. Remove the rose and apply some general-purpose fertilizer to the base of the hole.

APPLY MYCORRHIZAL FUNGI
Water the rose and leave to drain. Apply mycorrhizal fungi to the base of the hole, following the directions on the packet. The roots must come into contact with the fungi granules after planting, as these help the rose's root system to establish. Wearing gloves, tip the rose from its container and plant in the hole.

FIRM IN SOIL
Backfill around the root ball with excavated soil. Firm the soil with your hands to remove any air pocket. Water the rose well, then apply a 5cm (2in) layer of well-rotted organic matter, making sure that it does not touch the stems. Water the rose regularly during its first year, and apply a rose fertilizer each spring.

Enjoy some easy greens

There are fresh greens to be enjoyed from the garden all year round, providing a wonderful source of vitamins when there is not much else available. These are useful crops for filling gaps in the vegetable year, as they mature when others are either just starting to grow, or have finished for the season.

Spring cabbage

Spring cabbage is ready in late spring (earlier if grown as spring greens), when other crops are just getting going. Give it a sheltered position to help it survive the winter.

TOP TIP: REPEAT CROPPING

To harvest a succession of spring greens, start cutting in early spring, before the plants form hearts, cutting away the entire leafy part but leaving the stalk. Cut a cross in the top of the leftover stalks. This encourages the plant to sprout again, and produce a second flush of leaves, which you can then harvest. Do this to alternate plants in the row, leaving the others to form cabbages with rounded hearts.

 WHEN TO START
Late summer/early autumn

AT ITS BEST
Spring

TIME TO COMPLETE

 30 minutes sowing; 1 hour planting

YOU WILL NEED

 Spring cabbage seed
Seed compost
Pot
Modular seed trays
Dibber or garden trowel

1 SOW IN MODULAR TRAY
You can either sow seed directly in the soil and thin the plants later, or sow in pots and transplant into modules, planting the seedlings out once they have five leaves each. Water the soil well first.

2 PLANT OUT
Position plants 30cm (12in) apart for smaller spring greens; 45cm (18in) apart if you want fully-hearted cabbages. Do not add fertilizer – it encourages soft leafy growth, and your cabbages need to be tough to withstand the winter. In late autumn, mound up the soil around the stems to protect the plants during the worst weather. Spring greens can be harvested as soon as they are big enough to eat, while fully-hearted cabbages will be ready during the last month of spring.

Spinach

If you sow spinach every few weeks in spring and early autumn, and protect it over winter, you can harvest the tender leaves throughout the year.

 WHEN TO START
Spring or early autumn
AT ITS BEST
Summer

TIME TO COMPLETE
 1 hour

YOU WILL NEED
Spinach seed
A line of string
Trowel
Watering can

1 SOW IN DRILLS
Stretch out your string and use a trowel to make a shallow drill. Sow the seeds into it at 2.5cm (1in) intervals. Thin the seedlings to about 7cm (3in) apart for baby salad leaves, or 15cm (6in) apart for larger leaves to use for cooking. Protect seedlings in winter with a cloche (*see p.133*).

2 HARVESTING
You can cut the leaves when they are large enough to eat. Whether you remove individual leaves or cut off the entire plant, new leaves will emerge and give you a second crop. Regular watering can help prevent plants running to seed in warm weather.

Oriental greens

These are some of the most useful autumn vegetables, providing a hint of the exotic, just as the weather is cooling. They provide a great range of colours, textures and flavours, and can bring real variety to your salads and cooking.

WHEN TO START
Midsummer to early autumn
AT ITS BEST
Autumn

TIME TO COMPLETE
 1 hour

YOU WILL NEED
 Seed
A line of string
Trowel
Watering can

1 SOW SEEDS
Komatsuna, pak choi, bok choi, mizuna, mibuna and other Oriental greens are best sown in late summer, or they will quickly run to seed. They need a rich, fertile, moist soil. Sow *in situ* or in modules, thinning or planting to eventual spacings of around 15cm (6in).

2 PICKING THE CROP
Pick the leaves when young as a cut-and-come-again crop for salads and stir-fries, or leave them to mature fully and harvest the entire plant. If you cut the plant 2.5cm (1in) above the ground, it will produce a second crop of leaves.

Lay a gravel bed

Drought-tolerant plants that originate from arid, rocky places look most at home in a gravel garden. Ideal for a hot, sunny spot, a gravel border is easy to make, and can create a mosaic of colours and textures in areas where other plants struggle to survive.

 WHEN TO START
Spring

AT ITS BEST
Summer

TIME TO COMPLETE

 6 hours

YOU WILL NEED

 Drought-loving plants
Horticultural grit
Washed sand
Landscape fabric
Scissors
Galvanized staples
Watering can
Gravel
Boulders

1 PREPARE THE AREA

Dig over the area thoroughly and remove any weeds. You need a well-drained soil to keep drought-tolerant plants happy, so dig in washed sand and horticultural grit to make sure that yours drains freely, even in wet weather.

2 LAY MEMBRANE

Weed-suppressing membrane or landscape fabric allows rain to soak through to the roots, yet prevents weeds from growing. Lay it over the entire area, overlapping the edges, and pinning them down with galvanized staples as you go.

3 CUT CROSSES FOR PLANTS

Place your plants in their positions on the landscape fabric, and then arrange them to create a pleasing display. For each plant, cut a cross in the fabric, and fold back the flaps.

4 PLANT THROUGH FABRIC

Dig a hole and plant your plants at the same depth they were at in their pots. Add a little fertilizer to the back-filled soil, and firm it in. Replace the fabric to fit around the stems.

5 SPREAD GRAVEL MULCH

Once all of the plants have been watered in, spread a 5cm (2in) layer of gravel over the entire area. You may need to top this up occasionally to keep the garden looking its best. Water the plants in dry spells for the first year.

Self-seeded gravel garden

A slightly different style of gravel garden uses no landscape fabric. Plants are left to self-seed and create a wonderfully natural effect, but make sure you remove every scrap of perennial weed during the preparation.

ENCOURAGE SEEDING

Both weeds and seedlings of desired plants will spring up in a gravel bed, and it is important to learn the difference between them. You may have to allow weeds to grow larger than you would ideally like to identify them. In addition, take a relaxed approach to deadheading; seeds will never get the chance to form if the flowers are nipped off the moment they start to fade.

1 *Eryngium giganteum*; ↕90cm (36in) ↔30cm (12in) **2** *Meconopsis cambrica*; ↕45cm (18in) ↔25cm (10in) **3** *Nigella damascena* Persian Jewel Group; ↕40cm (16in) ↔23cm (9in) **4** Foxglove, *Digitalis purpurea*; ↕1.5m (5ft) ↔60cm (24in)

OTHER PLANTING OPTIONS

Alchemilla mollis	Nasturtiums
Alyssum	Shirley poppies
Aquilegias	Snapdragon
Eschscholzia	*Stipa tenuissima*
Feverfew	*Verbena bonariensis*

Grow scented sweet peas

The scent of sweet peas is like no other, and a vase of cut blooms filling a room with fragrance is reason enough to grow these cottage-garden favourites. In warm areas, sow seeds in the autumn; in colder parts sow in spring in a warm greenhouse or on a windowsill. Grow them on in an open, sunny area.

1 CHIP THE SEED
Sweet pea seeds have a hard shell, and unless water can penetrate it, the seeds will not germinate. To ensure the seed absorbs water, use a sharp penknife or nail clippers to carefully nick it opposite the "eye" (small, round scar) and remove a small piece of the seed coat.

2 SOW SEED
In autumn, fill trays or pots with seed compost and sow the seeds 1cm (½in) deep. Keep the seedlings in a cool greenhouse or cold frame until the following spring, only providing extra heat during severe frosts. In mid-spring, remove the tip of the main shoot from each seedling.

» WHEN TO PLANT
Autumn or early spring

AT THEIR BEST
Summer

TIME TO COMPLETE
 2–3 hours over several months

YOU WILL NEED
- Sweet pea seeds
- Sharp penknife or nail clippers
- Deep seed trays or root trainers
- Seed compost
- Well-rotted organic matter
- Obelisk or canes
- Garden twine
- All-purpose liquid feed

3 SEEDLING CARE
If you sow sweet peas in early spring, grow the seedlings indoors, or in a warm greenhouse, at 14–17°C (58–62°F). When they reach 10–15cm (4–6in) high, remove the tips down to the first set of leaves. Pinching out the tips like this encourages sideshoots to form.

Sweet pea supports

Sweet peas climb using their twining tendrils, which cling to slim supports, such as canes or sticks. These bushy plants reach up to 1.8m (6ft) high, so make sure your support is tall enough to accommodate them.

4 HARDEN OFF AND PLANT OUT
Autumn-sown seedlings can be planted out directly into the ground in mid-spring. Spring-sown seedlings will have tender shoots that need to be hardened off for a few weeks by bringing them outside by day, and inside at night. Plant hardened seedlings out in late spring.

5 PLANT CARE
Enrich the soil with well-rotted organic matter and plant one or two seedlings close to the base of a suitable support (*see right*) and tie them in loosely. The tendrils will soon take hold of the support as the plants grow. Water during dry spells, and apply a liquid feed every two weeks from midsummer. Pick the flowers regularly to encourage more.

TOP TIP: HOME-MADE SEED POTS

Roll folded newspaper around a glass and tuck the top ends into it. Remove, then flatten the tucked-in ends to form the base. Plant seedlings *and* their pots into the soil – the pots will just rot away.

BUYING SUPPORTS
Wooden or metal obelisks and tripods are ideal for sweet peas, and make decorative additions to flower borders or to vegetable beds, where you can plant them alongside runner or French beans. (Do not confuse the pods when harvesting, as sweet peas are poisonous). You may find that young plants struggle to take hold of smooth materials, such as metal, or do not cover the whole support evenly. To remedy this problem, wind some string around the poles and tie it horizontally across the legs of the support to provide the plants with more grip.

Elegant additions >
Stylish pyramids look stunning when dressed with a mix of sweet peas and runner beans.

MAKE YOUR OWN
It's easy to make your own sweet pea supports by setting out canes to form a wigwam and tying them securely at the top. Alternatively, grow them up pea sticks, or create a support with plastic mesh wrapped around a circle of sturdy canes driven into the ground, securing the trellis with garden twine or wire. As the plants grow, these supports quickly disappear beneath the flowers and foliage.

< Tunnel vision
This fragrant garden arch is made from metal poles and wire mesh, available from DIY stores, fixed at the top with wire. The sweet peas are scrambling over it to create a tunnel of flowers.

Create a year-round shrub display

Containers are not just for summer flowers; displays for autumn and winter often last longer and help to brighten up these cold, dark months when viewed from the warmth of your kitchen or living room. Make sure that the pot you buy can withstand low winter temperatures – frostproof clay pots tend to be more expensive but should come with a guarantee and last for many years.

WHEN TO START
Early autumn

AT ITS BEST
All year round

TIME TO COMPLETE

 1½ hours

YOU WILL NEED

Large frostproof container, at least
45cm (18in) deep and wide
Broken clay pot or polystyrene
pieces
Soil-based compost, such as
John Innes No.3
Mulching material
All-purpose granular fertilizer

Plants used in shrub display (left):
Skimmia japonica 'Rubella'
Juniperus 'Grey Owl'
Osmanthus heterophyllus 'Goshiki'
Erica arborea var. *alpina*
'Albert's Gold'

1 PREPARE THE POT

Add some broken clay pot or
polystyrene pieces to the bottom
of the container, and cover them with
a layer of soil-based compost. Set the
plants, still in their original pots, on the
compost and check that they will sit about
5cm (2in) below the rim when planted.
Keep them in the container, and start to
fill in around them with compost.

2 SLIDE THE PLANTS OUT

Pack damp compost around all
the pots up to their rims – only
one is shown here, but the method works
equally well with a few plants. Carefully
slide out the plants in their pots to leave
spaces for planting.

3 TIP PLANTS OUT OF THEIR POTS

Water all the plants well before
tipping them out of their plastic
pots. If the roots are congested, gently
tease them out. Carefully replace them
in their positions in the container, and
then firm more compost into any
remaining gaps.

4 ADD A MULCH

Add a layer of gravel, slate chips
or other decorative mulch over the
soil. Water the container well, and set it
on "feet" to allow the winter rains to drain
through easily. Place it where you can see
it easily from the house, and continue to
water it during the autumn and winter if
the soil under the mulch feels dry.

TOP TIP: ANNUAL CARE

The container will need watering
frequently in the spring and summer.
Each year in early spring, remove
the mulch and top few centimetres
of compost and replace it with fresh
compost mixed with some all-purpose
granular fertilizer. Water immediately
after this, and then renew the mulch.
When the plants become congested,
plant them out in the garden or move
to larger containers.

SELECTIONS >>

Shrubs for pots

Offering great value with their decorative foliage, sculptural forms and seasonal flowers, shrubs in containers are also fairly easy to look after, if you choose both container and plant carefully – a large pot will afford a greater choice of shrub and require watering less frequently than a small one. The plants here will all be happy in a container for a few years if you replace the top layer of compost and feed them annually each spring.

✸✸✸ fully hardy   ✸✸ hardy in mild regions/sheltered sites   ✸ protect from frost over winter
☼ full sun   ☀ partial sun   ☀ full shade   ◊ well-drained soil   ◐ moist soil   ● wet soil

1 *Rhododendron* 'Hydon Dawn'; ↕1m (3ft) ↔1m (3ft) ☼ ☀ (acid soil)◐ ✸✸✸   **2** Rock rose,
Helianthemum apenninum; ↕40cm (16in) ↔60cm (24in) ☼ ◊ ✸✸✸   **3** *Pieris japonica* 'Flamingo';
↕1.2m (4ft) ↔1m (3ft) ☼ ☀ (acid soil)◐ ✸✸✸   **4** Bay, *Laurus nobilis*; ↕1.2m (4ft) ↔45cm (18in)
if clipped ☼ ☀ (acid soil)◐ ✸✸   **5** *Hebe* 'Silver Queen'; ↕60cm (2ft) ↔ 60cm (2ft) ☼ ☀ ◊ ✸✸
6 *Fatsia japonica*; ↕1.2m (4ft) ↔1m (3ft) ☼ ☀ ◐ ✸✸   **7** *Hydrangea serrata* 'Bluebird'; ↕1m (3ft)
↔1m (3ft) ☼ ☀ (acid soil)◐ ✸✸   **8** Mock orange, *Philadelphus microphyllus*; ↕80cm (32in)
↔80cm (32in) ☼ ☀ ◊ ✸✸✸   **9** *Viburnum tinus* 'Variegatum'; ↕1m (3ft) ↔1m (3ft) ☼ ☀ ◐ ✸✸✸
10 *Lavandula* 'Willow Vale'; ↕60cm (24in) ↔60cm (24in) ☼ ◊ ✸✸✸

Seed a lawn

Sowing lawn seed is much cheaper than turfing, but you will have to wait a few months before it is ready for use. The best time to seed a lawn is in early autumn when the soil is warm and germination quick; sowing in early spring is an option but the colder soil conditions may prolong germination.

 WHEN TO START
Early autumn or early spring
AT ITS BEST
All year round

TIME TO COMPLETE
 3 hours or more for larger lawns

YOU WILL NEED
 Lawn seed
Well-rotted organic matter
Horticultural grit
All-purpose granular fertilizer
Canes or string
Pen and plastic cup
Bird-proof netting

1 CHOOSE YOUR SEED
Unlike turf, where you have a choice of just two or three types, lawn seed is available in many forms, including seed for shady spots or dry areas and clover lawns. Prepare the soil as for turf (*see p.32*). Mark out a square metre (yard) with canes or string, and weigh the right quantity of seed for that area. Pour the seed into a plastic cup and mark the top level with a pen. You can then use it as a measuring cup.

2 SOW SYSTEMATICALLY
Cover the soil evenly by scattering half the seed in the cup over the square metre (yard) in one direction, and then the other half at right angles. Set out the next square and fill the cup to the marked level; repeat the sowing process. Continue in this way until you have sown the whole area. If you have to walk over soil you have already seeded, stand on planks of wood to prevent your feet creating hollows in your new lawn.

3 PROTECT FROM BIRDS
Rake the seed into the soil to just cover it. Water with a can fitted with a rose, or spray lightly with a hose. Cover the seed with bird-proof netting, raised off the ground by about 30cm (12in). The seedlings should appear within 14 days; continue to water regularly. When the grass reaches 5cm (2in), make the first cut with your mower on a high setting. For autumn-sown lawns, maintain this height until spring, then lower the blades.

Lay a chamomile lawn

Sweet, soothing, scented chamomile has long been a desirable alternative to grass, and with the availability of turf, it is quick and easy to lay. Chamomile likes free-draining soil and, because it will not tolerate heavy wear and tear, is most suitable for decorative lawns, and fragrant seats.

 WHEN TO START
Early autumn or early spring

AT ITS BEST
All year round

TIME TO COMPLETE

 2 hours or more for larger lawns

YOU WILL NEED

 Chamomile turf
Well-rotted organic matter, such as farmyard manure
Horticultural grit
All-purpose granular fertilizer
Topsoil and horticultural sand

1 LAY THE TURF
Prepare your site as for turf, and if you have heavy clay, dig in lots of grit to ensure your soil drains freely; waterlogged soil will kill chamomile. Turf will consist of *Chamaemelum nobile* 'Treneague', a non-flowering, compact chamomile that spreads to form a dense mat. Lay the turf in the same way as grass (*see pp.32–33*).

2 CARING FOR CHAMOMILE
There's no need to mow chamomile because it naturally grows to just 6cm (2½in) in height. Trim it occasionally during summer, using garden shears to remove straggly growth and sideways spread. Pull out any weeds by hand before they have time to establish – do not use lawn weedkiller, as this will kill the chamomile. Each spring, apply a slow-release granular fertilizer and sprinkle a top dressing of sieved soil and horticultural sand over the lawn. Tread in the dressing to crush the stems, which promotes strong root growth.

Plant tasty tart fruit

Some fruits lend themselves to cooking. With the addition of a little sugar or honey, cooked rhubarb is transformed from super-sharp to pure nectar. Blueberries can be delicious raw, depending on how ripe they are, but their flavour really comes to life when they are baked in muffins or cakes.

Rhubarb

Once established, rhubarb looks after itself year after year. All you need do is pull as many stalks as you can eat.

>> **WHEN TO PLANT**
Late autumn

AT ITS BEST
Early summer

TIME TO COMPLETE

🕐 1 hour

YOU WILL NEED

 Rhubarb plant
Well-rotted organic matter, such as farmyard manure
Spade
Slug pellets or a slug ring

1 CHOOSE AN OPEN SUNNY SITE
Dig in organic matter, plant and water in well. Protect your plant from slugs, either using a copper slug ring or with a few slug pellets.

2 HARVEST STALKS
Water during dry spells. Feed every spring with an organic liquid fertilizer, and mulch with well-rotted manure. Do not pull any stalks the first year and only one or two in the second year. After that you can harvest more. To harvest, pull and slightly twist the stems.

TOP TIP: FORCING RHUBARB

Forcing rhubarb, by excluding all light when it first sprouts, results in sweeter, more tender stalks. As soon as you notice new shoots starting to appear in spring, cover the plant with a light-excluding barrier, such as a metal bucket, a box, or a rhubarb forcer, which will draw up the sweet stalks. The tender stems will be ready to pick about four weeks later – a month or so earlier than other rhubarb. Pick this crop, then leave the plant to recover for the rest of the year, and the following year.

Blueberry pots

These small, delicious berries are regarded as "super foods" because they are particularly high in vitamins and antioxidants. They need an acidic soil, and to guarantee fruit you should grow two different cultivars together.

» **WHEN TO PLANT**
Mid-autumn

AT THEIR BEST
Summer

TIME TO COMPLETE

🕐 1½ hours

YOU WILL NEED

🖊 Two blueberry plants
Two large pots
Broken clay pot pieces
Ericaceous compost and fertilizer
Mulch, such as bark chippings
Rainwater

1 PLANT IN LARGE POTS
Place broken clay pieces in the base of each large pot and part-fill with ericaceous compost. Plant the blueberry plants at the same depth as they were in their original pots, and fill in around the root balls with more compost, to within 5cm (2in) of the rim.

2 ADD FERTILIZER
To ensure a good crop, add a slow-release ericaceous fertilizer to the compost, following the instructions on the packet. Most slow-release fertilizers last for a limited period, so re-apply as specified. Don't use non-ericaceous fertilizers, as these could harm your plants.

3 WATER AND MULCH
As tap water often tends to be alkaline, use rainwater to water the plant thoroughly. Then place a mulch of bark chippings over the compost to help retain moisture. Water daily with rainwater. The berries will ripen over a few weeks; pick as required.

Plant a climber

Create a wall of flowers and foliage by clothing your boundaries and other vertical surfaces with beautiful climbers. The planting method shown here is ideal for twining climbers (*see opposite*) and roses that need some support; ivy and other self-clinging plants will not require wires.

 WHEN TO START
Autumn or early spring
AT ITS BEST
Summer, for honeysuckle shown

TIME TO COMPLETE
 2 hours

YOU WILL NEED
 Climber – honeysuckle, *Lonicera periclymenum* used here
Screwdriver
Plastic-coated wire
Vine eyes
Well-rotted organic matter
All-purpose granular fertilizer
Bamboo canes
Garden twine
Bark chipping mulch
Spade and trowel

1 WIRE UP YOUR SURFACE
Screw parallel rows of vine eyes, 45cm (18in) apart, into wooden fence posts (use a drill and Rawlplugs in concrete posts). Fix horizontal wires between each row, and turn the vine eyes a few more times to tighten the wires.

2 DIG A PLANTING HOLE
Dig a hole twice as wide and a little deeper than the plant pot, about 45cm (18in) from the fence or screen. Place the plant in its pot in the hole to check the planting depth.

3 INSERT CANES
Place the bamboo canes in the hole at the edge closest to the fence or screen. Arrange the canes into a fan shape and attach them to the horizontal wires. These will provide the climbing plant with a temporary support until it reaches the wires. The canes can then be removed but take care not to break any stems that have wrapped themselves around them.

4 POSITION THE PLANT
Water the plant, then remove it from its pot. Place it in the hole and lean it towards the fence; ensure the root ball is not above the soil surface. Add fertilizer to the excavated soil and backfill.

5 CREATE A RESERVOIR
Using some of the surrounding soil, form a circular ridge around the base of the climber to create a saucer-shaped depression. This acts as a water reservoir, and guides moisture to the roots.

6 FINAL TOUCHES
Tie the stems loosely to the bamboo canes with garden twine. Water the plant and mulch with organic matter or chipped bark, keeping it clear of the stems. Water regularly throughout the first year, especially during dry spells.

Choosing climbers

Climbers have developed a variety of means to adhere to vertical surfaces, and understanding what method your chosen plant uses will help you to provide the right support. Use the examples below as a guide.

HOW CLIMBERS CLIMB

Some climbers attach themselves to surfaces without requiring additional support. These include ivy (*Hedera*), which clings using aerial roots, and Virginia creeper and Boston ivy (*Parthenocissus* species), which use adhesive pads. Plant self-clingers with caution, as they can damage old or weak brickwork. Roses climb using their thorns to hook onto taller plants, and unless you grow them through a host plant, they need support from horizontal wires or trellis. Clematis, sweet peas, passion flower (*Passiflora*), and honeysuckle (*Lonicera*), among others, use twining stems or tendrils to climb, and are best supported by canes or wires thin enough for them to wrap around, or by growing them through a host plant.

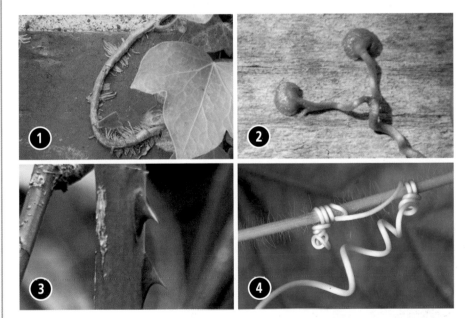

❶ Ivy climbs via aerial roots ❷ Virginia creeper grips with adhesive pads ❸ Roses hook their thorns onto supports ❹ Passion flower tendrils grasp whatever is in reach.

SELECT THE RIGHT SUPPORT

Check the final height of your chosen climber, and select a support that will be large and strong enough for a mature plant. As an alternative to wires (*see left*), you can tie smaller climbers directly to trellis, or a bought, or home-made obelisk (*see pp.134–136*). Threading climbers through shrubs or trees takes up no extra space, but offers a dual effect – perfect for small plots.

Clematis for all seasons

Thread these climbers through trees and shrubs or grow them over arches and pergolas for colour from spring to autumn. Their fluffy seedheads then steal the show in winter, making clematis a must for any garden. Choose a selection, starting with spring-flowering, scented *armandii* and *montana*, followed by 'Vyvyan Pennell' and 'Bees' Jubilee' in early summer, with the remainder providing dazzling colour from midsummer to autumn.

❋❋❋ fully hardy   ❋❋ hardy in mild regions/sheltered sites   ❋ protect from frost over winter

☼ full sun   ☀ partial sun   ☀ full shade   ○ well-drained soil   ◐ moist soil   ● wet soil

❶ *Clematis* 'Ville de Lyon'; ‡2–3m (6–10ft) ☼ ☀ ◐ ❋❋❋   ❷ *Clematis* 'Etoile Rose'; ‡2.5m (8ft) ☼ ☀ ◐ ❋❋❋   ❸ *Clematis* 'Vyvyan Pennell'; ‡2–3m (6–10ft) ☼ ☀ ◐ ❋❋❋   ❹ *Clematis* 'Bill MacKenzie'; ‡7m (22ft) ☼ ☀ ◐ ❋❋❋   ❺ *Clematis henryi*; ‡3m (10ft) ☼ ☀ ◐ ❋❋❋   ❻ *Clematis montana* var. *rubens* 'Tetrarose'; ‡5m (15ft) ☼ ☀ ◐ ❋❋❋   ❼ *Clematis* 'Bees' Jubilee'; ‡2.5m (8ft) ☼ ☀ ◐ ❋❋❋   ❽ *Clematis* x *diversifolia*; ‡2–3m (6–10ft) ☼ ☀ ◐ ❋❋❋   ❾ *Clematis armandii*; ‡3–5m (10–15ft) ☼ ☀ ◐ ❋❋   ❿ *Clematis* 'Purpurea Plena Elegans'; ‡3m (10ft) ☼ ☀ ◐ ❋❋❋   ⓫ *Clematis* 'Ascotiensis'; ‡3–4m (10–12ft) ☼ ☀ ◐ ❋❋❋

SELECTIONS »

Lawn care

A verdant lawn makes a wonderful foil for flower borders and creates an emerald focal point in winter when colour is in short supply. There are different types of turf for different situations but all lawns benefit from regular mowing, and care and attention in the spring and autumn.

MOWING AND WATERING

Mow grass whenever it is growing, provided the ground isn't too wet or icy to walk on. In spring, mow once a week with the blades at their highest setting, and gradually lower them as growth accelerates. Use a box to collect the clippings, which can be composted, or use a "mulching mower" which doesn't remove the grass but chops it into fine pieces, returning nutrients to the lawn. Rake off thick patches of clippings, which will damage the turf. In summer, a high-quality lawn may need cutting three times a week, but in autumn, as growth slows, once or twice a week should suffice. In dry periods, water newly laid turf, freshly sown areas, and high-quality lawns. Leave established lawns unwatered, but stop mowing, as longer grass helps protect the roots. The grass may turn brown, but will recover once rain returns.

< When to water
Water a new lawn every week in dry spells, until it is established. You can tell when fine lawns need watering as they lose their spring when walked on. Reduce water evaporation by using sprinklers early in the morning or at night. Move seep hoses by 20cm (8in) every half an hour.

FEEDING

The amount of fertilizer you need to maintain lush green grass depends on how rich the underlying soil is, and if you occasionally leave the clippings on the lawn, which help top up the soil nutrients. Apply granular or liquid lawn fertilizer at least once a year. Spring and early summer feeds are high in nitrogen to boost leaf growth; products for use in early autumn are low in nitrogen but high in potassium to aid grass roots in winter. Do not overfeed as this can result in weak growth and fungal problems.

∧ Applying fertilizer
Divide the lawn into a grid of metre squares using canes. Apply fertilizer at a rate according to the pack. Hire a calibrated spreader for large lawns, and water if it doesn't rain within three days after feeding.

TOP TIP: HOME-MADE TOP DRESSING

Applying a sandy top dressing (*see opposite*), helps to rejuvenate lawns, especially those grown on heavy soils, by increasing drainage and encouraging strong root growth. Mix your own dressing by spreading out a sheet of plastic close to the lawn. Then, using a bucket as a single measure, combine three parts good-quality top soil or sandy loam with six parts horticultural sand and one part peat substitute, such as coir or ground composted bark. Let the mixture dry slightly so you can spread it more easily, and then work it thoroughly into the surface of the lawn.

Autumn treatment

After a summer of heavy use many lawns start showing signs of wear and tear by the end of the season. Early autumn is a great time to repair the damage and to ensure that your turf is in good condition for the year ahead.

1 RAKE OUT MOSS
Kill off any moss with a lawn moss herbicide before vigorously scratching out dead material (thatch) from the lawn with a spring-tined rake; hire a motorized scarifier for large lawns. Raking improves the look and health of the turf.

2 AERATE THE SOIL
Open up air channels in a compacted lawn by pushing a border fork into the soil, or use a hollow tiner, which pulls out plugs of soil. Work across the lawn at 10cm (4in) intervals. Repeat this process every two years.

3 APPLY TOP DRESSING
After raking and aerating the lawn, work a top dressing into the holes. You can buy this premixed from garden centres and DIY stores, but it's easy and cost effective on large lawns to make your own (*see Top Tip, opposite*).

4 BRUSH IN DRESSING
Work in the top dressing thoroughly using a stiff brush or besom, lightly filling the new aeration channels, and covering the ground to encourage strong rooting. Apply it evenly and make sure the grass isn't smothered.

5 FEED AND SOW
Wearing gloves, apply a granular autumn lawn fertilizer evenly over marked out squares (*see Applying fertilizer, opposite*). Water in if no rain falls within three days of applying it. In early autumn, the soil is sufficiently warm and moist to sow grass seed too. Sprinkle seed to match your lawn type at half the recommended rate for new lawns to help thicken up any bald spots.

TOP TIP: WEEDING OPTIONS

Acidic lawns are prone to moss and weed growth. Check soil pH in winter, and raise it by applying ground chalk or limestone at a rate of 50g per sq metre (2oz per 10 sq ft). Apply a lawn weedkiller in spring or summer, and repeat in early autumn to remove any remaining weeds. Organic gardeners can grub out creeping buttercups, daisies (*below*), and tap-rooted weeds, like dandelions, using an old knife.

Plant bare-root bamboo

Bare-root bamboo plants are significantly cheaper than those grown in pots, and are a good option if you need several to create a screen, as shown here. You may also get a bare-root plant if a friend has sections to spare. Plant them as soon as you get them home to prevent the roots drying out.

WHEN TO PLANT
Autumn
AT THEIR BEST
Summer

 TIME TO COMPLETE
1–2 hours

 YOU WILL NEED
Bare-root bamboo
Plastic bag
Spade
Compost
Watering can
Root barrier
Garden moss

< *Elegant screen*
Bamboo makes a perfect screen to hide ugly objects in the garden or to ensure privacy. Evergreen, clothed in foliage all the way up the stem, and with an upright habit, it takes up less space, if controlled, than the average hedge.

1 KEEP ROOTS MOIST
As the roots are not in soil and will dry out and die very rapidly, you must keep them moist before planting. Place a plastic bag filled with garden moss around the roots, and keep the moss damp until the last minute, when you are ready to plant.

2 ADD ORGANIC MATTER
Dig a hole larger than the rootball and break up the base using a fork. In the bottom, add a layer of well-rotted organic matter, such as garden compost or farmyard manure, and mix it in lightly. Add more organic matter to the excavated soil from the hole and mix this together.

3 PLACE BAMBOO INTO HOLE
Unwrap the bamboo, gently tease out the roots and carefully lower it into the planting hole. Keeping the plant upright, add the organic matter and soil mix, firming down as you go to make sure there are no air pockets between the roots.

4 PLANT AND FIRM IN BAMBOO
Fill in the hole around the stems, making sure the plant is at the same level as originally planted. To do this, look for an earthy tidemark on the stems, showing where the soil had previously come up to. Firm well and water.

5 AFTERCARE
Keep the immediate area weed-free while the plant is establishing. Water regularly during dry spells to ensure the plant roots do not dry out. Thin out and tidy established clumps every two years in early spring, before they begin shooting. Cut any dead or weak stems down to ground level.

TOP TIP: CONTROLLING BAMBOOS

Some bamboos are "runners" and once established will send out roots all over the garden. These plants need containing with a root barrier made from a non-perishable material, such as rigid plastic or slate. Dig a narrow trench round the clump and insert your barrier. Cut and remove all peripheral roots, then fill in with soil.

Carpets of colour

Create spectacular effects, even on a small scale, by naturalizing bulbs in a lawn or under trees. Choose robust plants able to compete with roots and grass: snowdrops, daffodils, or crocuses (*shown here*) are ideal. Leave them to their own devices and they will gradually spread, year after year, to form a beautiful flowering carpet.

 WHEN TO PLANT
Autumn

AT ITS BEST
Early spring

TIME TO COMPLETE

 1–2 hours

YOU WILL NEED

Spring bulbs – between 15–25 bulbs per 30cm (12in) square
Slim trowel or bulb planter
Spade
All-purpose granular fertilizer

1 PREPARE THE GROUND
In autumn, remove any perennial weeds, such as dandelions and daisies, and mow the grass. Since bulbs dry out quite quickly, aim to plant them as soon as possible after buying them. When planting, choose a fine day when the soil is not waterlogged or frozen.

2 PLANTING RANDOM GROUPS
To achieve a random, natural effect, toss the bulbs into the air and plant them individually where they fall. For each bulb, dig out a small plug of soil and turf, 2–3 times the depth of the bulb, with a slim trowel or bulb planter. Add a little fertilizer, plant the bulb, and replace the soil plug.

3 PLANTING IN SMALLER GROUPS
For smaller groups of bulbs, cut an H-shape into the grass with a sharp spade. Holding the spade horizontally, slice under the turf and fold it back to reveal the soil. Remove more soil for larger bulbs, such as daffodils. Add a little fertilizer and plant the bulbs. Cover with excavated soil and gently fold back the flaps. Water well.

Rake up a leafy conditioner

Leafmould is one of the finest soil conditioners, and makes excellent use of a resource that is free and abundant in autumn – fallen leaves. All you need to make rich, crumbly leafmould is a plastic bin liner, some leaves from deciduous trees and a good dollop of patience.

» **WHEN TO START**
Autumn

AT ITS BEST
The following autumn

TIME TO COMPLETE
 1 hour

YOU WILL NEED
 A rake
Leaves
Plastic bag
Hand fork
Watering can

1 RAKE UP FALLEN LEAVES
When leaves start to fall in autumn, rake them up. For larger supplies, collect leaves from local parks or woods, but do not use those close to main roads.

2 PLACE IN A PLASTIC LINER
You can make a leafmould bin, but a plastic bin liner works just as well and has an added advantage, which is that it can be kept in a small space, such as behind a shed. Put leaves into the liner, pushing them down as you go.

3 SPRINKLE WITH WATER
As you pack the leaves in, occasionally stop and sprinkle them with water. Wet leaves will rot down much quicker than dry ones. Keep filling and wetting until the bag is full. One bag of leafmould won't go very far, so try to collect enough leaves to fill a few.

4 TIE BAG SECURELY
Your bag is going to be left for a long time, so make sure you tie it up well. This will prevent small creatures making a home in the leaves.

5 PUNCH A FEW AIR HOLES
Leaves also need air to rot down efficiently, so punch some holes in the sides with a fork. Put the bag away and forget about it for at least a year.

TOP TIP: USING LEAFMOULD

After a year or two, your leafmould will be ready to use. It works particularly well as a mulch, and is especially loved by woodland plants. Alternatively, it can be sieved and used as an ingredient in potting compost.

Nature's helpers

Inside a wormery, worms break down kitchen waste and turn it into rich compost. They can even cope with scraps, such as cooked food. Wormeries are available from specialist suppliers.

TIME TO COMPLETE
🕐 1½ hours

YOU WILL NEED
A wormery, with tigerworms included
Food waste
Soft "bedding" such as coir or shredded newspaper

1 ADD THE WORMS
Place the tigerworms on the bedding, then start by adding a small amount of food waste (referring to the pack instructions). Worms take a week to settle in and get up to full speed. Do not add any more food during this time.

2 FEED YOUR WORMS
After the settling in period, you should be able to use most of your food scraps, making sure you add some every day. It is best to use a variety of food and other ingredients, such as leaves and moist newspaper, to ensure the texture does not become too dense. Worms can cope with most foods, but they struggle with citrus fruits and meat.

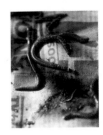

3 FINAL COMPOST
Wormeries can become acidic, so occasionally add lime, such as calcified seaweed. When the compost is ready it will be dark, fairly soggy and slightly spongy. The worms are just below the surface, so can be easily removed. You can then use it on garden borders or mix it in with your other compost.

Dramatic amaryllis

Hippeastrum (commonly known as amaryllis) provide the biggest, boldest flowers of winter, and can even be bought pre-forced, so that they bloom in time for the Christmas holidays. For such exotic-looking blooms, their needs are simple: a nice tight pot, water, light, and a short rest in late summer is all they require.

⟫ WHEN TO PLANT
Autumn

AT ITS BEST
Winter

🕐 **TIME TO COMPLETE**
A few hours during the year

YOU WILL NEED

1 *Hippeastrum* bulb
Basin
Multi-purpose compost
Container
Balanced liquid fertilizer

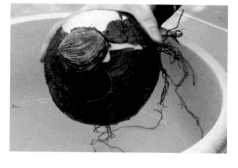

1 SOAK BULB
Soak the bulb roots in a basin of lukewarm water for a few hours. This will soften them, and encourage the bulb to come into growth again.

2 PLANT IN CONTAINER
Choose a pot, just larger than the bulb itself, that has a drainage hole. Fill the base with compost, place the bulb on top, and add more compost. Leave the top third of the bulb protruding.

3 LEAVE TO SHOOT
Water the bulb well to help settle the compost, then place the pot in a bright, warm spot at about 21°C (70°F). Water sparingly until new leaves appear; then water regularly, keeping it moist.

TOP TIP: REPOTTING BULBS

Hippeastrum go into dormancy at the end of summer. If yours doesn't, stop watering and feeding it, and cut back the leaves to encourage it to do so. Repot into a slightly larger pot. After several weeks, when new growth appears, resume watering.

∧ A firm hand
Ensure the bulb is firmly planted so that it does not topple over when in flower.

4 AFTERCARE
Turn the pot frequently to prevent the flower stalk growing to one side. Move the plant to a cool spot when it starts flowering, to prolong the display. Feed weekly after flowering.

Flower choices

Hippeastrum are excellent festive plants, and offer an equally vibrant alternative to the traditional poinsettias. They usually flower in shades of red and white, but some have orange, salmon, and even green-tinted blooms. Their large trumpet-shaped flowers are often heavily patterned, and vary greatly in shape; some are broad and round, while others are slender and elegant.

❶ 'Lucky Strike' is an early-flowering cultivar with deep red, rounded flowers that make a particularly festive choice for a Christmas windowsill. ❷ 'Apple Blossom' is scented, with pink-blushed, white flowers. Each bulb produces several spikes, with around four flowers apiece. ❸ 'Giraffe' has slender cream petals, decorated with vivid red stripes and splashes. It usually flowers about ten weeks after planting. ❹ 'Prelude' is possibly the most spectacular of all the *Hippeastrum*, producing an abundance of huge red and white flowers on tall, upright stems. It usually flowers in as little as five weeks after planting.

Plant a formal hedge

Yew, hornbeam, and beech make excellent closely-clipped hedges, and you can reduce the cost by buying young bare-rooted plants from late winter to early spring from specialist nurseries and growing them on yourself. Prepare your soil in advance and plant immediately, unless the soil is frozen or waterlogged.

≫ **WHEN TO PLANT**
Late autumn to early spring

AT ITS BEST
All year round

TIME TO COMPLETE
 4 hours or more depending on hedge size

YOU WILL NEED
 Young bare-rooted hedging plants (yew, *Taxus baccata*, shown here)
Well-rotted organic matter, such as farmyard manure
Spade
Fork
Canes
Garden string
Watering can or hose
All-purpose granular fertilizer

1 PREPARE THE SITE
Six weeks before planting, remove all weeds from the site and dig a trench the length of the hedge and 1m (3ft) wide. Fork in organic matter, and refill the trench. Set out a line to mark the edge of the hedge.

2 MARK PLANTING INTERVALS
Dig a trench twice as wide and as deep as the plants' root balls. Using a ruler or guide, lay canes at 45–60cm (18–24in) intervals along the string line to mark the planting distances.

3 CHECK PLANTING DEPTHS
Check that the plants will be at the same depth as they were in the field when planted – you will see the soil line just above the roots. Place one plant by each cane, and backfill around the roots with soil, removing any air gaps with your fingers.

4 FIRM IN WELL
When in place, check that the plants are upright and then firm in around them with your foot. Create a slight dip around each plant to act as a reservoir, and water well. Add a thick mulch of compost or manure, keeping it clear of the plant stems. Water for the first year and feed plants annually in spring.

Using pot-grown plants

Some plants, such as lavender, box, holly, and privet, are not generally available in bare-root form and are grown and sold in pots. The planting technique is similar to that for bare-root types but pot-grown hedging can be planted at any time of year, as long as the soil is not frozen or very dry.

» WHEN TO START
Any time; early autumn or spring is best

AT ITS BEST
All year (evergreen)
Spring to autumn (deciduous)

TIME TO COMPLETE
3 hours or longer depending on hedge size

YOU WILL NEED
Pot-grown holly plants, *Ilex aquifolium*
Well-rotted organic matter, such as farmyard manure
All-purpose granular fertilizer
Spade
Fork
Canes
Garden string
Watering can or hose

1 DIG PLANTING HOLES
Prepare the soil and mark out the area as in Steps 1 and 2 opposite. Either dig a long trench or individual holes for each plant – holes need to be twice as wide and as deep as the root ball.

2 TEASE OUT ROOTS
If planting in spring, add some fertilizer to the excavated soil. Tease out any congested roots before planting at the same depth as the plant was in its original pot. Firm in with your foot and water well. (*See Step 4 opposite for aftercare.*)

Frost protection

Some plants and containers need a little help to get them through cold winters but they can be left outside if you provide some protection when temperatures dip below freezing.

The big cover-up

Tender plants must be brought inside in winter because they die when exposed to freezing temperatures, but those that can survive a few degrees of frost (given two stars in this book) should survive outside in all but the coldest regions.

PLANTS TO PROTECT

Many slightly tender plants survive low temperatures but not cold, wet soils, so ensure yours drains freely before planting. Other plants are not killed by frost, but their flowers may be damaged. Examples include peach trees, magnolias, and camellias, which suffer when frosted blooms thaw too quickly in warm morning sun. Young leaves and buds of hardy plants can also be sensitive to frost, so don't feed in late summer because it promotes this vulnerable new growth. Also, allow herbaceous plants to die down naturally so that the leaves fall over the plant, creating a protective blanket, and apply a thick mulch over those that may suffer in low temperatures, like *Alstroemeria* or diascias.

∧ Ice-laden maple
Acer palmatum *cultivars are hardy, so just enjoy the sparkle of their vibrant deciduous autumn leaves laced with frost.*

∧ Straw blanket
Use chicken wire to secure a straw blanket over frost-sensitive plants that prefer dry soil conditions.

< Star fright
The flowers of star magnolias are damaged by frost; protect them with garden fleece.

TOP TIP: OVERWINTER BANANAS AND TREE FERNS

Popular for tropical gardens, *Musa basjoo* is one of the hardiest bananas and tolerates winters outside if protected from cold, wet conditions. First, cut down the stems and remove the leaves. Attach chicken wire to bamboo canes set around the plant to form a cage, and pack it with straw. Treat tree ferns in the same way: make a cage around the plant, fold the fronds over the top of the stem, and pack straw around it.

∧ Make a waterproof hat
Both bananas and tree ferns suffer in wet winters, so top the wire cage with a waterproof covering, such as clear plastic sheeting. In very cold regions you can also add a fleece wrapper. Remove the protection in late spring or when you see new growth.

Cloches for crops

Some vegetables that overwinter in the soil benefit from a protective cloche or a layer of straw. Likewise, crops that are sown early in spring may grow more quickly if kept snug when frosts strike. A wide variety of cloches is available to buy, or make one yourself from recycled materials.

CHOOSING A COVER

Winter root crops, such as parsnips, carrots, and leeks are difficult to lift when the soil is frozen, so cover them with a layer of insulating straw in autumn. Cold frames are ideal for spring-sown frost-hardy seedlings in trays or pots, which will be transplanted outside later in the year, while a cloche is best for crops that are sown *in situ* in early spring, such as lettuce, rocket, and Oriental greens, or for overwintered vegetables like broad beans.

Cloches can be bought ready-made and as kits, or if you want frost protection for just a few weeks each year, a home-made type constructed from a few sheets of clear plastic may suffice. Alternatively, make a more permanent tunnel from wire hoops covered with clear polythene; leave one end open for ventilation.

∧ *Shop-bought option*
Cloches are an investment and should last for many years; choose from pricey decorative glass types to cheaper plastic models.

< *Home-made solution*
This cloche is easy to make with two sheets of clear plastic pinned together with pegs.

Wrap up your pots

Container plants can suffer in winter on two fronts: roots are more vulnerable in pots because they afford less insulation than the soil in the ground, and the pots themselves may crack or break during icy periods.

CONTAINER CARE

Some containers are more vulnerable to frost damage than others. Stone, metal, and plastic pots will sail through winters unscathed, while terracotta often cracks in frosty conditions. Terracotta suffers because it is porous and when moisture from the soil and rain leaches into it and then expands as it turns to ice, the pot cracks. So, unless you pay a premium for containers that have been fired to high temperatures to reduce their porosity, you will need to take steps to ensure yours stay intact. Either remove plants and compost and store pots inside, or, if they are housing a prized plant, wrap them up with hessian or bubble plastic. Cover the compost, too, so that it does not become saturated. Another tip is to line the pot with bubble plastic before you plant it up, thereby forming a barrier between the soil and the terracotta.

Slightly tender potted plants are best wrapped in horticultural fleece in the winter. Also tie together the leaves of strappy plants, such as cordylines, to protect their crowns from snow and ice.

∧ *Pot protection*
Line terracotta pots with bubble plastic to prevent them absorbing moisture and cracking when the water turns to ice in cold weather.

< *Hessian wrapper*
Wrap tender plants and vulnerable pots with hessian or bubble plastic to keep them warm.

Make an obelisk for climbers

Timber obelisks suit almost any garden design, be it formal or a relaxed country-cottage style. Use them draped with clematis or other flowering climbers to add height to a border, as a feature to flank an entrance, or to create a focal point at the end of a walkway. Top-quality wooden types are expensive to buy, but you can make one yourself for a fraction of the cost, if you have reasonable DIY skills.

 WHEN TO START
Any time
AT ITS BEST
Depends according to planting

TIME TO COMPLETE

 1½ hours

YOU WILL NEED

 4 x 2.5m pieces of 34mm x 34mm
   timber for uprights
2 x small offcuts of timber for
   template
25m of 34mm x 9mm batten,
   cut into short lengths for
   horizontal struts
Offcuts of 75mm x 25mm timber
   for top plinth
1 x decorative finial
Galvanized 34mm screws
Drill with countersinking bit
Screwdriver
Saw
Non-toxic wood stain or timber
   preservative

1 MAKE A TEMPLATE
First, make templates for the sides. Drive two screws halfway into a timber offcut, 12cm (5in) apart, for the top of the obelisk. Drive two more screws halfway into a second offcut, 50cm (20in) apart, for the bottom. Lay both offcuts parallel to one another, 2.4m (8ft) apart. Place two upright timbers between them to create a quadrangle shape.

2 CREATE THE SHAPE
Bring the top ends of the upright timbers up against the screws in the top offcut template, as shown. Repeat at the other end of the timbers, butting these up against the screws in the bottom offcut template.

3 SCREW IN A BATTEN
The uprights now form a fat triangular shape. Take a piece of batten and lay it across the uprights, 30cm (12in) from the bottom ends. Using the drill with the countersinking bit, make holes in the batten and uprights, and screw them together.

4 ATTACH A PLINTH
In the same way, place a small offcut for the plinth at the top of the two uprights (narrow end). Make four holes, two in each upright, and screw the plinth into place to secure the top.

Clematis cladding >
To help clematis climb this obelisk, tie garden twine between the struts for the tendrils to cling to.

continued...

5 FINISH THE BATTENS

Following the instructions in step 3, screw more battens in place at 15cm (6in) intervals, from the base to the plinth, to create a triangular, ladder-like structure.

6 TRIM THE ENDS

Using a saw, trim the battens flush with the sides of the uprights. Repeat Steps 2 to 5 to create a second ladder-like structure and trim the battens. Treat both with a wood stain or preservative.

7 FIX SIDES TOGETHER

Fit the two sides of the obelisk into the two templates, as shown here. Then, screw in a piece of batten between the two sides to start forming the third side, lining it up with the existing battens. You may find this easier if someone holds the structure to keep it stable.

8 FINISH THE SIDES

Work your way up the third side, screwing the battens carefully into place, and then repeat the steps for the fourth and final side. Trim all the battens as described in Step 6.

9 CUT THE CAP

Screw in offcuts to complete all four sides of the plinth. Measure the top and cut a square to fit. Stain it and, when dry, screw it into place in each corner to form a cap.

10 FIX ON FINIAL

Wooden finials are available in various styles. Here, we have used an acorn. Stain the finial and screw it to the centre of the cap.

11 FINISHING TOUCHES

To complete the project, stain the remaining battens and touch up any missed areas. The stain or wood preservative will prevent decay and prolong the life of the obelisk. Reapply it every couple of years in early spring before clematis and other deciduous climbers come into growth. Secure the obelisk in place, either by burying the bottom 10cm (4in) of the structure in soil, or by using proprietary fence post supports.

Plant a clematis

Their elegance, colour, variety and exquisite flower shapes have catapulted clematis to the top of the climbers' charts. Plant them with care and you will enjoy these superstars for many years to come.

∧ **Shade the roots**
Choose a site where the clematis roots will be shaded, and the flowers can reach the sun.

» WHEN TO START
Early autumn

AT ITS BEST
Depends on variety

TIME TO COMPLETE
🕐 1½ hours

YOU WILL NEED
🔹 Clematis plant
Well-rotted organic matter, such as farmyard manure.
Spade and fork
All-purpose granular fertilizer
Bamboo cane
Wires and vine eyes (if planting next to a wall or fence)
Garden twine

1 PREPARE THE GROUND
First, dig plenty of organic matter into the soil. If growing clematis up a wall or fence, position the plant 45cm (18in) away from it. Dig a hole about 30cm (12in) deep, fork over the base, and add some fertilizer to the excavated soil.

2 CHECK THE DEPTH
Clematis are best planted deeply, so that if clematis wilt strikes, the plant will survive. Place the clematis in its pot in the hole, and lay a cane over it to check that the lower stems will be 5cm (2in) beneath the soil surface when it is planted.

3 PLANT AND BACKFILL
After watering thoroughly, remove the clematis from its pot and plant it in the hole. Carefully backfill with the fertilized soil, pushing it gently between the brittle stems with your fingers and making sure there are no air pockets as you go.

4 AFTERCARE
Gently firm the soil with your foot, and tie stems to an obelisk or other support. Water in well. Add a thick mulch of well-rotted organic matter, keeping it clear of the stems. Continue to water regularly until the plant is established.

Perfumed pendants

Big and beautiful, wisteria is the queen of climbers. Some would consider growing it for its gnarled, twining growth and graceful, green foliage alone, but then in early summer, it tops all this by producing a truly breathtaking display of long, pendant, scented flowers. All it needs is a little annual care.

CHOOSING PLANTS

Wisteria is notorious for being slow to flower, but this is only if it is grown on its own roots. Whereas plants grown from seed may take over ten years to start flowering, grafted ones can bloom within three or four years. The nursery or garden centre should be able to reassure you about this, and you can see the graft yourself at the base of the stem, but the best way to be sure is to buy a plant in flower. The open flowers also give you the chance to decide exactly which colour you prefer.

PLANTING AND SUPPORT

Wisterias are big, heavy climbers, so only plant them where you have a large, sturdy support in place such as heavy-duty wires or a pergola. Prepare the soil well before planting, digging it over and mixing in plenty of organic matter (*see pp.116–117 for planting advice*). At first you may need to tie the stems loosely to their supports, but this task won't be necessary for long as they begin to twine (*see right*).

Pruning care

Wisterias should be pruned twice a year to encourage them to flower well.

 WHEN TO PRUNE
Winter and summer

TIME TO COMPLETE
 3 hours

YOU WILL NEED
 Secateurs
Ladder
Organic matter
Twine

1 **SUMMER PRUNING**
The best time to assess the overall shape of your plant is after flowering. If there are any gaps, fill these by training new stems along the support in that direction. Tie this new growth in loosely to the framework using twine.

2 **REDUCE NEW SHOOTS**
Once stems are tied in, cut back all other growth to about 30cm (12in) from where it sprouts. Restricting growth, and allowing sunlight and air to ripen the young stems helps to promote flowering the following year.

3 WINTER PRUNING

For best results, prune again in late winter. First identify any long, sappy stems that sprouted after pruning in summer, and prune them back to about five buds away from the main branch, cutting just above a bud.

4 SPUR PRUNE

Then, shorten the shoots that were pruned in the summer even further, back to two or three buds. Look carefully for the fat, round flower buds, and avoid cutting these off. Foliage buds, which can be removed, are slimmer and pointed.

5 KEEP PLANTS IN CHECK

Wisteria is a vigorous plant, and its stems can become thick and woody with age. These can cause problems if they grow where they are not wanted, so cut stems away from gutters, windows and behind pipes when you are pruning.

Cover up for winter

Cold, dark winter days can be depressing, but with a few well-chosen climbers to dress up your screens, boundaries, and bare-stemmed trees, this can be an exciting and beautiful season. Bright, variegated foliage, sunny yellow flowers, and sweetly scented blooms are among the delights in store.

Ivy arch

Often overlooked or dismissed as too common, ivy comes into its own in winter, with beautiful leaf shapes and bright colours. Grow it over an arch for a spectacular foliage effect.

 WHEN TO START
Autumn

AT ITS BEST
All year, especially winter

 TIME TO COMPLETE

 1 day to make arch; 1 day to plant

YOU WILL NEED

Garden arch (kits are available)
Well-rotted organic matter, such
 as farmyard manure
Garden twine
Secateurs
Ivy plants, good choices include:
 Hedera helix 'Cavendishii',
 'Glacier', 'Oro di Bogliasco', and
 Hedera colchica

1 ERECT AN ARCH
When bold foliage is at a premium, ivy has plenty to offer, with plain or variegated, and large or small leaves. Select a tall cultivar of *Hedera helix* or the large-leaved *Hedera colchica* for an arch. Either buy a pre-assembled arch, or make one from a kit and erect it close to a screen, over a bench seat, or to frame a view.

2 PLANT THE IVY
Select an ivy with long stems, and check the label to make sure that it will grow large enough to cover the arch. Enrich the soil around the arch with organic matter, and plant an ivy about 30cm (12in) away from each side. You can also plant a few 30cm (12in) from the fence or wall. Plant the ivies at the same depth they were in their original pots.

∧ **Winter greens**
This beautiful arch, covered with variegated ivy and flanked by evergreen Euonymus *and bay, creates a show-stopping winter focal point.*

3 AFTERCARE
Use garden twine to tie the stems to the arch; they can be removed once the stems have taken hold. Water the plants frequently and trim any wayward stems in spring and summer.

Seasonal gold

The winter jasmine, *Jasminum nudiflorum*, is really a wall shrub, but its long, lax stems are easily trained over trellis or on wires to cover screens and fences. Masses of starry golden yellow flowers appear on bare stems in late winter and early spring, but unlike summer jasmine, they are unscented.

PLANTING JASMINE

Choose a spot that will be in full sun or partial shade in the winter to encourage the best blooms. Note that areas that are in sun in summer may be shaded later in the year, so check your aspect carefully. In autumn, dig well-rotted organic matter, such as farmyard manure or home-made garden compost, into the soil before you start, and plant the jasmine as for wall shrubs.

∧ > *Frosted flowers*
Winter jasmine's tough little flowers continue to bloom even when dusted with frost. During dry spells, keep the plant well watered until established, and feed with a shrub fertilizer each spring.

Evergreen clematis

Exquisite blooms set amid evergreen foliage are the star qualities of winter-flowering clematis. Plant them in a sheltered site as they won't tolerate very low temperatures.

PLANTING TIPS

Clematis armandii has sweetly scented white or pink flowers and long, slim, dark green leaves. In some areas it may stay quite compact, but when fully established and in a suitable location, it can romp through a large tree. *Clematis cirrhosa*, with its freckled, cup-shaped flowers, can be equally vigorous in ideal conditions. Although these clematis are less likely to fall prey to clematis wilt, it is still worth planting them deeply in well-drained soil, just in case the disease strikes.

AFTERCARE

Water well during dry spells for the first year until the plants are established, and clip untidy growth lightly after flowering. The lower leaves of *Clematis armandii* may turn brown and fall, which is a characteristic of this plant; use another climber or shrub to disguise the stems.

∧ *Freckled friends*
The flowers of Clematis cirrhosa *var.* purpurascens *'Freckles' appear throughout the winter.*

Winter delights >
Stunningly beautiful, the flowers of Clematis armandii *emit a delicious scent, and appear for many weeks from late winter to early spring.*

Silver splash

Begonias come in many forms, and these elegant foliage types make handsome features in a modern indoor arrangement (*right*). Choose tall simple containers to contrast with the heavily textured leaves, partner them with small-leaved trailing plants, and set them in a line or up a few steps.

>> **WHEN TO START**
Any time
AT ITS BEST
All year round

TIME TO COMPLETE
 2 hours

YOU WILL NEED
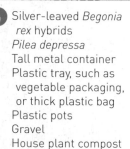
- Silver-leaved *Begonia rex* hybrids
- *Pilea depressa*
- Tall metal container
- Plastic tray, such as vegetable packaging, or thick plastic bag
- Plastic pots
- Gravel
- House plant compost

1 LINE THE CONTAINERS

If your container has drainage holes, place a deep plastic tray in the bottom to prevent water leaking out, or line it with a thick plastic bag. Then add some gravel to the bottom. Also buy plastic plant pots that fit neatly into the container.

2 ARRANGE THE PLANTS

Cover the drainage holes of the plastic pots with gravel, top up with compost, and plant the begonias and *Pilea* (one in each pot). Water and allow to drain. Arrange the pots in the container, adding more gravel to raise them up to the correct level, as required.

Caring for begonias

Begonia rex hybrids come in many colours and forms, but all require the same treatment. Feed them fortnightly in summer and once a month in winter, and keep them away from bright sunlight to prevent the foliage from scorching.

FOLIAGE NEEDS

Although they dislike strong sun, begonias produce the best colours in bright, diffused light, and prefer a temperature of 18–21°C (64–70°F). Watering is the key to success, since they are prone to rotting if given too much or too little. Every two weeks, remove the plastic pots from the container, and place them in a bowl of water that reaches just below the rims. Allow moisture to seep up from the bottom, and when the top of the compost is wet, take them out and leave to drain.

Begonias come in an array of spectacular colours and forms. Specialist nurseries offer the widest choice, and most offer a mail-order service:

❶ 'Martin Johnson'
❷ 'Benitochiba'
❸ 'Tiny Bright'

Acknowledgments

Dorling Kindersley would like to thank the following people (2010 edition):
Andrew Halstead and Beatrice Henricot from RHS Wisley Gardens for their help with the pest and disease section.
Project Editor Caroline Reed **Editors** Chauney Dunford, Becky Shackleton **Additional text** Jenny Hendy
Senior Designer Lucy Parissi **Designer** Francesca Gormley **Picture Research** Jenny Baskaya, Lucy Claxton
Managing Editor Esther Ripley **Managing Art Editor** Alison Donovan
Publisher Jonathan Metcalf **Art Director** Bryn Walls.

Picture credits

The publisher would like to thank the following for their kind permission to reproduce their photographs:
(Key: a-above; b-below/bottom; c-centre; f-far; l-left; r-right; t-top)

6 Getty Images: picturegarden (cr). **7 GAP Photos:** Brian North (bc). **Photolibrary:** Nicholas Rigg (tl). **11 Getty Images:** GAP Photos (br). **13 Getty Images:** GAP Photos (cr) (fcr). Marianne Majerus Garden Images: Marianne Majerus (br). **15 GAP Photos:** Paul Debois (tl). **20 Getty Images:** Christina Bollen (t). **22 GAP Photos:** Richard Bloom (ca). Getty Images: Lee Avison (crb); Richard Bloom (bc). **23 GAP Photos:** Richard Bloom. **28 Alamy Images:** John Glover (tr). **32-33 Dorling Kindersley:** Design: Nigel Boardman & Stephen Gelly, Hope Begins at Home, RHS Hampton Court 2009. **35 GAP Photos:** Friedrich Strauss. **38 Brian T. North:** (l) (r). **39 Brian T. North:** (tl) (cl) (tr). **40 Marianne Majerus Garden Images:** Marianne Majerus (cb). **41 Getty Images:** Christina Bollen (t). **42 Getty Images:** Mark Turner (l). **45 Caroline Reed:** (tr). **46 Harpur Garden Library. 47 Harpur Garden Library:** (bl). **53 GAP Photos:** Friedrich Strauss (t). **56-57 GAP Photos:** Jo Whitworth. **58 Photolibrary:** Gary K Smith. **61 Getty Images:** Pernilla Bergdahl (cr); Keith Burdett (b); Clinton Friedman (t). **62 GAP Photos:** Howard Rice (t). **68 Getty Images:** Will Heap (cra). **69 Getty Images:** Foodcollection RF (bc) (cb); Michael Grimm (tl); Gregor Schuster (tr). **73 Getty Images:** Hugh Palmer (pebbles). **79 Dorling Kindersley:** Courtesy of the Royal Botanic Gardens, Kew (l). **83 Dorling Kindersley:** Design: James Mason & Chloe Gazzard, The Path Not Taken, RHS Hampton Court 2007 (tr). GAP Photos: Jonathan Buckley, Design: Simon Hopkinson, Location: Hollington Herb Nursery (crb). **84 Dorling Kindersley:** Design: Jon Wheatley, Mary Payne & Terry Porter, The Growing Tastes Allotment Garden, RHS Hampton Court 2009 (bl). Getty Images: JGI/Jamie Grill (br). **85 Dorling Kindersley:** Design: Amanda Yorwerth (tr). **87 Getty Images:** Richard Bloom (cl). **91 Marianne Majerus Garden Images:** Marianne Majerus/Longacre, Kent (l). **95 Getty Images:** Richard Bloom (l). **98 Getty Images:** Mark Bolton. **100 Dorling Kindersley:** Design: Jeff Hewitt, Jacob's Ladder, RHS Chelsea 2009; www.hewittlandscapes.co.uk. **104 GAP Photos:** Clive Nichols, Design: Clare Matthews (cr). **105 GAP Photos:** Juliette Wade (tr). **107 Getty Images:** Howard Rice (bl). **108 GAP Photos:** Graham Strong. **112 Alamy Images:** The Garden Picture Library. Dorling Kindersley: Design: Mike Harvey & Arun Landscapes, The Unwind Garden, RHS Hampton Court 2007 (cra). **113 Dorling Kindersley:** Design: Robert Myers, The Cancer Research Garden, RHS Chelsea 2008 (t). **115 Caroline Reed:** (clb) (cb) (crb). **116 Getty Images:** Richard Bloom (t). **117 Photolibrary:** Rex Butcher (crb). **120 Getty Images:** Nigel Cattlin (cla). **122 Dorling Kindersley:** Design: Koji Ninomiya & Takumi Awai, A Japanese Tranquil Retreat Garden, RHS Chelsea 2009. **123 Caroline Reed:** (br). **129 Getty Images:** Clive Nichols (ca); Polina Plotnikova (cb) (crb). **130 Dorling Kindersley:** Design: Luciano Giubbilei, Laurent-Perrier Garden, RHS Chelsea 2009 (t). **132 Getty Images:** Clive Nichols (t). **133 Getty Images:** Nicola Browne (cra). **138 Caroline Reed:** (cra). **139 The Garden Collection:** Jonathan Buckley – Design Judy Pearce (t). **140 GAP Photos:** S & O. **141 GAP Photos:** Howard Rice (tr); Richard Bloom (clb). Getty Images: Jonathan Buckley (cla). **142 Getty Images:** DEA/C.DANI (br).

All other images © Dorling Kindersley
For further information see: **www.dkimages.com**